D1345081

GREAT SEX GAMES

ANNE HOOPER

GREAT SEX GAMES

ANNE HOOPER

A Dorling Kindersley Book

Dorling Kindersley

LONDON, NEW YORK, SYDNEY, DELHI,
PARIS, MUNICH and JOHANNESBURG

Designed and edited by
Focus Publishing

Senior Managing Art Editor	Lynne Brown
Senior Managing Editor	Corinne Roberts
Senior Art Editor	Karen Ward
Project Editor	Claire Cross
DTP	Rajen Shah
Production	Liz Cherry

This edition published in 2000 by
Dorling Kindersley Limited, 9 Henrietta Street,
Covent Garden, London WC2E 8PS

A CIP catalogue record for this book is
available from the British Library.

ISBN 0 7513 2904 5

Reproduced by GRB Editrice Srl. Italy
Printed by L.E.G.O. Italy

see our complete catalogue at
www.dk.com

CONTENTS

GREAT SEX GAMES
Introduction

The sexiest relationships I have enjoyed were those where trust and excitement were so profound that my partner and I felt we could do absolutely anything in bed. "Anything" included spontaneous lovemaking, routine lovemaking (nothing wrong with that), and playing at sex games.

I didn't arrive at games playing until I had gained confidence, but I'm very glad I got there. I've had fun – I wouldn't have missed it for anything. Yet, to begin with, it wasn't easy to

play. I found it difficult to understand that if games are going to remain erotic you have to stay firmly in the character that the game decrees. Everything depends on not being allowed to change your mind halfway through. For example, if you suddenly stop being strong and instead become wimpish, the illusion is instantly shattered. And good sex games are all about creating illusion and stirring up the imagination.

So, to aid and abet every potential Games Master or Mistress, I have outlined in this little book a few potent tips to get the blood running and the juices flowing (figuratively speaking, of course).

HOW THE BOOK WORKS

Like any game, a sex game must have rules. It cannot function without them. So the first section of the book looks specifically at what it is that you hope to get out of games playing. And it lines up some basic rules that are absolutely necessary to ensure what you are going to do is both effective and safe.

The first games are low-key and promote the growth of acceptance and trust. These are followed at various points throughout the text by "Scenarios." Scenarios are sexual stories that you might like to act out with your lover or quite simply read out loud in bed on a warm summer's afternoon. The later games involve using sex toys, punishment and reward systems, mild restraint, and fetishistic specialities. In order to practice punishment and reward, you need to be familiar with some pretty powerful incentives. I outline these in my final chapter and hope that they go a long way toward completely blowing your mind – not to mention other parts of your body.

I don't believe that it is only unusual people who play sex games. I think the most ordinary among us naturally play like children when we are with someone we adore. I simply offer a few fun ideas for sex games. If you want to take them on board, I hope you have a great time. If you don't, I just hope you have an enjoyable read.

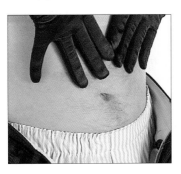

THE RULES OF THE
Game

Without rules there can be no game. This doesn't mean that you are forced to state the rules formally between the two of you. However, it does mean that you must establish the limits of a game clearly to *yourself*, must be prepared to stick to them whatever happens, and must not hesitate to talk them through with your partner when it is clearly necessary.

THE AIM OF
The Game

The idea of a Games Master/Mistress comes directly from the darker caverns of erotica. Every dominatrix is a Games Mistress. Every male commanding sex "slaves" is a Games Master. It need not be so extreme, but the concept of the Games Master/Mistress is a good one.

First, it implies that someone is in charge, which can be reassuring to nervous beginners. Second, becoming Games Master or Mistress is the basis of some entertaining gaming in itself. Third, in order to be a Master or Mistress you need to be trustworthy and dependable – not perhaps the qualities you may have first thought of. Men and women who play sex games are often more trusting than couples with more traditional relationships.
So here are the aims and the rules of the game.

YOUR AIMS

What you want to promote

- Your partner's trust.
- Your partner's excitement.
- Your partner's eager anticipation.
- Your partner's X-rated imagination.
- Reassurance that your own behavior is acceptable.
- The self-belief that you can lead the game well.
- Your own arousal.
- Truly imaginative ways to experience sex.

What you want to prevent

- Scaring your partner.
- Taking your partner too far, too fast.
- Hurting, or in any way threatening, your partner beyond what you have established is mutually acceptable. In many countries sexual activities that involve physically hurting others, even if they are consenting adults, is illegal.
- Losing control of yourself when you are the Games Master/Mistress.

ESTABLISHING A CODE WORD

If you are playing a sex game in which your partner is at your mercy, you may be making a mistake if you stop the action the first time your partner asks you to do so. This is because although your partner may be a little scared, they may also be delighted at the same time. The two emotions often go hand in hand. "Stop, stop," can actually sometimes mean "This is amazing, please *don't* stop." So how can you tell when you really ought to stop?

The solution to the problem is to establish a code word. This can be a word that you have agreed to beforehand that indisputably means "Stop right now." The minute the code word is uttered, you must always stop immediately.

However, using a code word is really only suitable between lovers who know each other well. In a first-time sex situation, actions of this kind could well be interpreted as aggressive.

YOUR ACTIONS

Moves you may make

• You may:
touch; fondle; caress; stroke; offer fantasies;
ask for fantasies; use sex toys.

• With your partner's consent you may:
establish a safety code word; dominate;
submit; use light bondage; tempt; tickle;
tantalize; photograph; use sex toys;
tell tall stories.

Moves you may not make

• Take the action beyond the agreed limits.

• Disregard a partner's use of the safety
code word.

• Expose a partner publicly (and this includes
showing photographs of your sexual activities
to others).

• Bring in any third party (unless this is by
firm mutual consent).

• Physically or emotionally hurt or damage
your lover.

GAINING EACH OTHER'S TRUST

As we discuss the use of safety code words in
sex games, it becomes clear that in order for
any "safety agreement" to work, you and your
partner must trust each other implicitly.
Without complete trust, sex games simply do
not work. There's not a lot of point in setting
up elaborate safety precautions if deep down
you fear your wishes will be disregarded in
any case. If you are tense and nervous, your
own sexual experience will be at best poor and
at worst threatening. In such circumstances,
the first rule of the game is: DON'T DO IT.

YOUR FIRST MOVES

Your own personal rules

Establish your own trustworthiness in the earliest
days of the relationship by stopping any activity
the minute your partner indicates that this is
what they want. (By this I am not advocating
restraint games – I am stressing the importance
of setting up trust at the very outset.)

Introduce your partner to aspects of your world other than sex. Let them see you in the context of your friends, and of your friends' good opinion of you. *The more you open up to them, the more secure they will feel.* Think "honest" to yourself. In order for someone to find you reliable, you actually must *be* reliable.

What your partner should be able to expect

- That you see them as a separate, vulnerable human being.
- That you will ask them about their feelings.
- That you will truthfully state details about yourself. If you are nervous, say so. But be positive as well, saying something like: "The truth is that I haven't done much of this kind of thing before. But I get a strong sense from knowing you that this is going to feel great."
- That you will give your partner time if that is what they want. The more laid back you are about getting into sex games, the more your partner will trust you.

LOSING YOUR
Inhibitions

If you want to be a sex games player, you need to possess a fair degree of self-confidence. In order to feel completely free with your lover, you need to believe that the actions you make are acceptable. The moves on the following pages are designed to help you lose inhibitions and establish a sense that anything you do with your lover is great by them!

TAKE THINGS
Gently

Games players are often bolder and more dramatic than romantic lovers. And since drama doesn't come spontaneously to everyone, this next section outlines some possible preliminary interests.

SETTING THE SCENE

It's not just your own actions that make a sexual encounter special – it can be the ambience of the room that you are using. A gothic bedroom with an iron four-poster bed and blood-red drapes is naturally going to make a stronger impact than a shabby room, with a broken-down wardrobe in one corner and a chair with one leg missing in the other.

REHEARSAL IS GOOD

If you feel nervous, remember that rehearsal helps. There is no law to say that you can't take time to explore your fantasies. You might start by simply talking them through. That way, you will feel safe. And when you see that nothing awful happens, then perhaps you will be a little bolder next time.

Just because you rehearse something sexually doesn't mean that it must be artificial. In fact, if it feels that way, then you may need to take things very slowly indeed. The whole point about anything sexual, be it quick or slow, is that it should feel wonderful.

Going into new sex ideas slowly, so that they are graduated, is a way of reassuring both yourself and a nervous lover. After all, most people do look for "hand-holding" as they discover new sexual layers to their personality.

Action tip

Always remember – nobody has to play any sex game they dislike. You can say "NO!", right from the outset.

EROTIC BODY
Confidence

One of the best sex skills that you can learn is the art of truly letting go. This means feeling completely at home in your body and focusing exclusively on the erotic sensations that you are giving and receiving.

SEXUAL SELF-CRITICISM

We often worry about what we look like during sex. Rather than giving ourselves up to the moment, an inner voice says things like, "I must look ridiculous!" We can fall into the trap of feeling anxious about how we smell, taste or even sound. All of these concerns can diminish our sexual repertoire so that:

- we stop making love with the light on
- we stop making love in certain positions
- we may refuse sexual acts that we enjoy because we feel self-conscious.

LOVE YOUR BODY

The answer to this problem is twofold. *First*, make an effort to keep your body in the best possible shape. Make an objective assessment of your body and then decide if you want to change anything. But remember: never try to conform to idealized media images of attractiveness. Simply aim for small improvements that will make you feel sexually confident.

Second, if you can't change anything, then learn to love your body exactly the way it is. If you do this, your partner will feel the same. People always respond to those who are positive. Being open and uninhibited are two of the sexiest qualities a person can possess. Also, ask yourself if you ever really scrutinize your partner's body during sex? If you don't, then isn't it highly unlikely that they will do it to you?

SEXY
Dressing

When dressing for sex, the rules are simple. Wear tight clothes that emphasize the curves and contours of your body and draw the eye to the genitals, chest, or buttocks. Clothes should be extremely difficult to take off (the idea being that you tease your partner into submission while remaining inaccessible), or extremely easy to remove.

LOOK THE PART
If you are going to play sex games, you want to look and feel sexy at the outset.

24

Subvert your normal dress codes: if you dress down in your everyday life, dress up for sex. If you normally dress very conservatively, dress provocatively. Shocking your partner by wearing something unexpected always has erotic power. Add realism to fantasies by dressing the part – devote a special part of your wardrobe to sex games. If (as a female) you usually wear pale, quiet cosmetics, try experimenting with deep crimson lipstick. Huge dark lips are seen as universally sensual. And guys, don't forget, some women love men who wear eye shadow.

THROW A FANCY DRESS PARTY
The condition of entry is that guests must dress as their favorite sexual fetish or fantasy.
- Tight, short leather – anything made of leather – has sado-masochistic overtones.
- Fake fur – this suggests decadence, especially if you are naked beneath a fake fur coat.
- Uniforms – symbols of authority are always sexy. Dress up as a policeman, fireman, doctor, nurse, or teacher. Servant and schoolgirl uniforms suggest servility and innocence.
- Cross-dressing – try to create at least a moment's uncertainty as to your true gender.

FUN WITH SEXY
Underwear

Underwear has an important symbolic value
in that it is the last item of clothing you
remove before sex. When underwear is silky
and sexy, it can have a wonderful aphrodisiac
effect, making you feel great and ensuring that
your partner is longing to get their hands on you.

SEXUAL SHORTHAND

As with any costume, underwear can help you
play a sexual role with conviction. If you are
a woman and you want to play innocent
and virginal, choose pure white underwear
in silky fabrics. Confidence and experience is
conveyed by black suspenders, stockings,
panties, and bra. If you want to make a
brazen statement of lust, wear a red bustier.
Use underwear as a sexual shorthand to tell
your partner what kind of sex you want.

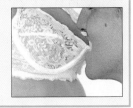

Undressing tip
Take off each other's underwear with your teeth. The only thing you're allowed to use your hands for is her bra clasp.

Men have fewer types of underwear to choose from but, nevertheless, should not get complacent about underclothes. Instead, buy something your partner will find attractive. Black, silk boxer shorts are a good start. If you don't know what she likes, try the following exercise.

EROTIC UNDERCLOTHES
Draw up a list with your partner of the types of underwear you find sexy and those that you cannot stand. Something like:
Sexy:
• Tight shorts (men & women) • See-through bras
• Black straps • Lycra • Bright white underwear
Unsexy:
Stars & Stripes boxer shorts • Anything yellow • Socks
• Tights • Strap marks

SEXY
Undressing

If you're not used to stripping, the following exercise can help. Stand in front of a full-length mirror, pretend that you're alone and very slowly take off all of your clothes. Take time to really look at your body in the mirror and touch yourself in whatever way you want to.

DELIBERATE PROVOCATION

Women If you are completely comfortable undressing for your partner, aim for deliberate teasing. Look him in the eye and slowly remove each garment, caressing your skin as you go. When you are wearing only your underwear, tease him by

For added eroticism
If it makes you feel better, or less shy, let your man hide in the next room and watch you around the side of the door.

slowing down the
pace even more.
Finally, turn
your back on
him, and slip
your panties off.

Men There is a right
way and a wrong way of getting
ready for sex. Take it slowly. Don't end
up stark naked except for your socks.
The best way is to undress each other, even
if you end up ripping the clothes off.

TIPS FOR STRIPPING
• Avoid garments that you have to pull over
your head.
• Don't wear tights or socks.
• Drop each garment on the floor as you
take it off.
• Wear sexy underwear that your partner
has never seen before.

MAKING THE BODY
Erotic

Wear a piece of erotic jewelry under your clothes and ask your lover to undress you. Or give erotic jewelry as a sexy present. Choose a toe ring, ankle bracelet, navel decoration, or waist chain. You can even buy genital jewelry.

EROTIC PIERCING

There is a generation of people who associate body piercing with sexual feelings. A ring through the nipple, they say, feels sensual to them and fascinates their partner. Piercing is certainly an excellent way to draw attention to a particular part of the body, such as navel, lip, tongue, or eyebrow.

TO TATTOO OR NOT TO TATTOO

A tattoo is a major commitment – once the skin has been injected with indelible dye, you gain a body adornment that lasts for a lifetime. Nevertheless, many people enjoy the psychological thrill of having a tattoo. Hidden tattoos, on the inner arms, thighs, and buttocks can be sexy discoveries for lovers to make. Even the genitals can be tattooed.

Less permanent options are henna tattoos or those that last for just a few days and can be removed with oil. You can even have temporary tattoos custom-made. Give your lover a surprise: apply a temporary tattoo and then tell them that you have a secret on your body that only they can find.

THE TATTOO AS ART

Tattoos are regarded by many people as works of illustration. When you see some of the amazing Japanese "body suits," you get an inkling as to why they might believe this. One heavily tattooed man even went so far as to stipulate that when he died his skin should be removed so that it might go on permanent display!

GETTING SEXY WITH
Body Paints

Good sex often contains an element of humor, and using body paints is a wonderful way to have fun, explore your partner's body, share intimacy and eroticism, and revert to childhood all at the same time. Not to mention feeling great afterward!

USE YOUR HANDS AND FINGERS

Use paints that are designed for use on the face or body, and if you don't have any, improvise with lipstick. Don't worry about using a paintbrush – the sensual pleasure of dipping your fingers in the paint is part of the experience. Or you can cover

your hands in paint and leave hand prints all over each other. Afterward, bathe together and soap each other's painted body all over.

NIPPLE PAINTING
Nipples are one of the most sensitive places to body-paint.

GAMES

- Use glow-in-the-dark paint and turn the lights off.
- Give your partner a sex change: paint breasts on him and a penis on her.
- Paint a fruit platter on your partner's body, using the curves and contours of the body to suggest the fruits.
- Paint her nipples and then take prints on a blank sheet of paper.
- Draw patterns on her buttocks and then get her to sit on you.
- Blindfold your partner and then color-code different parts of their body. Ask them to choose a color and then stimulate that area.
- Write a sexual favor on your partner's back, but don't deliver it until they guess what it is.
- Lick off edible paints.

SENSUAL

Massage

The skin is the body's most under-exploited sex organ. Massaging your partner is a unique way to feel close, give and receive blissful sensations and kindle passion. Massage can be a sensual exercise in its own right or a prelude to sex. You don't need any special skills in order to perform sensual massage – just your hands and a vivid imagination.

ASSEMBLE YOUR MASSAGE PROPS

Make a props box for massage games. This is rather like a children's toy box except that, instead of toys, you fill it with a diverse assortment of fabrics, household items, and other tactile objects. Pick objects that feel soft and comforting, such as silk scarves, feathers, soft make-up brushes, and furry fabrics but also include things that provoke novel sensations. For example, a rubber glove, a hairbrush, a rolling pin, a pumice stone, a tennis ball, a furry paint roller (clean!), some smooth pebbles, some plastic food wrap, a ribbon, a string of beads, a pin, a fork, a piece of leather, and some PVC. Now you're all set to test your partner's sensory skills.

A SENSORY VOYAGE

Ask your partner to lie down and put on a blindfold so that he concentrates exclusively on the sensations he is about to receive. Tell him that he is going to be treated to a tactile feast. Start by stroking him with a make-up brush on his temples, then his buttocks, then the soles of his feet. The "massage" that follows should be as diverse and creative as possible. For example, drag the fork lightly across his chest;

test his sensitivity to tiny pin-pricks all over his body; caress his genitals with the rubber glove; use the hairbrush to brush his pubic hair; press the pebbles into the palms of his hands, massage the backs of his thighs with the rolling pin. Try touching his genitals with all these different objects.

Make your massage as interactive as possible. Ask questions such as:

"Can you feel this?"

"Can you feel it here?"

"Do you like that?"

"Which do you like best?"

Part of the fun of the massage is asking the recipient to guess what the massage toy is (and seeing his face when he finds out later on).

It's also an opportunity to discover which parts of your lover's body are most and least receptive to different types of touch – valuable information that you can store up and use later when you make love.

MASSAGE – THE BASICS

The only guidelines for giving a massage are: keep your hands in contact with the skin as much as possible, ask for feedback, and don't do anything that hurts. You can make your massage strokes good and smooth by using massage oil on your hands. Ask your partner to lie naked on a warm towel.

You don't need an expert's repertoire of strokes to give a good massage: just remember to use deep kneading pressure on muscular areas such as the shoulders, back, buttocks, and thighs, and gentle feathering strokes on delicate areas such as the face, joints, and belly. If in doubt, use a gentle gliding stroke with flat hands all over the body.

LEARNING TO ENJOY
Self-Touch

Believe it or not, self-touch is a good way of learning to feel confident – or at least, confident in yourself. Therapists working with women experiencing difficulty reaching orgasm found that the more they got to know their bodies and sexual responses, the more certain the women felt about other aspects of their lives.

Here's how to proceed. Prepare in advance. Make sure you have a warm, comfortable room, and above all, complete privacy. Think about any erotic props that you would like to use: a book of sexual fantasies, massage oil, a sex toy, or simply a glass of wine. Then make sure these are close to you.

TAKE IT SLOWLY

Don't be in a rush to undress – start by touching yourself through your clothes and concentrate on the various sensations in a way that you may not have time to with a partner. Rather than touching your genitals straight away, caress your lips, neck, nipples, and belly with your fingertips.

TEASE YOURSELF

Slowly undress yourself. Put some massage oil on your hands and explore the contours of your body. If you find areas of muscle tension, knead them away with your hands. Stroke and rub your pubic area and buttocks, but don't actually touch your genitals. Keep yourself aroused by touching erogenous areas of your body then start to fleetingly touch your genitals. Focus on the sensations all over your body and listen carefully to your breathing. Make a noise if you feel like it and let your mind wander into erotic fantasy. Now concentrate more on your genitals, but resist the

urge to masturbate to orgasm. If you are getting too excited, slow down. Pretend that you are teasing a lover. In this way, keep yourself on the brink of orgasm for 20–30 minutes.

AFTERPLAY

When you have reached orgasm, don't jump up and get dressed. Instead, lie back and enjoy the post-orgasmic feelings of relaxation. Close your eyes and concentrate on breathing deeply. Move your palms in big circles around your belly and, if you feel like it, drift off into a light sleep.

CHANGE YOUR ROUTINE

Be experimental when you masturbate. Do things that you wouldn't normally do. Touch yourself with different

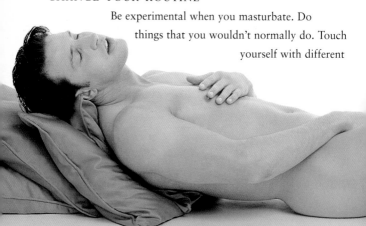

Action tips

Think of the session as an act of self-love. Believe that you deserve every erotic sensation that you can give yourself. Don't just obediently stroke your skin. Make this an occasion for giving yourself a sensual time in many ways – hence the suggestion of a drink. You might like to put on gorgeous music, or curl up on a sheepskin rug. Don't hesitate to add massage oil or a vibrator, if that is what you would like.

textures – a silk scarf or a string of beads. Masturbate in front of the mirror, looking at yourself from different angles. Cover yourself in oil. Put your fingers in your mouth and explore your tongue and the insides of your cheeks. Describe what you are doing out loud. Masturbate with the other hand. Do it in an unusual place. Be inventive with household props. And remember that no-one's watching you.

SHARING
Fantasies

Sharing a fantasy is the best sort of spontaneous sex game.
There are lots of ways of acting out the blue movies of your
imagination: you can wear costumes, you can decorate your
bedroom, or you can rely purely on imagination and role-play.

Get together with your partner, and discuss the fantasies that
you enjoy, those that you are ambivalent about, and the ones
that you dislike. This helps establish the
ground rules for game-playing. Be
completely honest, but also be non-
judgmental. You can explain to
your partner that you don't want
to try a particular fantasy, but
don't criticize their sexuality.
Also, if your fantasies
focus on
someone
who is

not your lover, tread with caution. Although you may know
that you have no intention of sleeping with your new colleague
at work, you can easily make your partner feel insecure.

ENACTING FANTASIES

Choose a favorite sex scene from a film, such as the food scene
in *9½ Weeks*, and re-enact it in the same place with the same
props. Watch your sex scene in a mirror for a cinematic effect.
Write down different fantasy roles or characters on pieces of
paper. For example, slave, teacher, virgin, or
prisoner – or maybe someone famous –
and then interact in character.
Pick a fantasy theme and decorate
your bedroom in that style – maybe
an oriental boudoir, a *Kama Sutra*-
style palace bedroom, a bedouin tent
or a den full of sex toys.

EXPLORING TABOOS

Some people worry that their fantasies
are a sign of a deviant sexuality. For
instance, fantasies about the same sex,

or sex involving force, can make people feel worried about their unconscious motives. Actually, the most common explanation for fantasies is that we are naturally drawn to things that we perceive as forbidden, naughty, or taboo. However, although these taboos are erotic in our imaginations, we don't usually want them to happen in real life, because they would probably affect the "safe," everyday images that we project. If you have a fantasy that you are nervous about, here is a game to help you.

Fantasy swapping

Revealing fantasies takes courage. We may fear shocking our
partner or being the object of humor, ridicule, or even disgust.
The way to overcome this is to make a pact to take turns to
swap fantasies. Start gently, and progressively spice up your
fantasies. The only other rule is that your respective fantasies
must be of equal "value". For instance, if your partner
describes an exotic fantasy, then yours must be equally wild.

COPING WITH FEARS

Choose one "strand" or aspect of your fantasy and explain it
to your partner. The strand you choose should be symbolic and
should capture the most erotic aspect of your fantasy. For
example, if you fantasize about being forced to have sex by a
stranger, tell your partner that you want him to make love to
you when you are least expecting it and that he must continue
his seduction even if you protest. Don't forget: it is vital to
build rules into games like this. Always have a pre-arranged
code word that either of you can use at any point
if you want the game to stop. (See *The Rules of
the Game*, on page 14.)

CREATING
Scenes

Most of us think of bedrooms as just places to sleep. Big mistake. For places to sleep are not at all the same as places in which to have sex. The atmosphere is seriously different.

GOTHIC RITES

Focus your imagination on a black wrought-iron four-poster bed festooned with deep blue drapes that tumble over the struts and wind around the posts. The lighting is strictly candle power, wax dripping

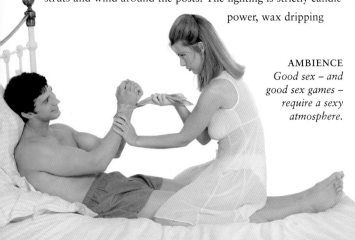

AMBIENCE
Good sex – and good sex games – require a sexy atmosphere.

from a silver candelabra while a red shade is pulled down across the window. What do you feel as you peer in, half-hidden by the gloom? Anticipation? Curiosity? Fear? Already your pulse is racing and your mind roars through a series of darker possibilities. You are a little aroused

before another move is made. For a sex game in an atmosphere like this, you might pretend to be a monk and a novice nun.

MOORISH IMAGES

We gain ideas of sensuality from what we see around us. If you find yourself in a Turkish room, for example, draped with the purples and reds of the desert, a low platform bed and layers of brightly colored rugs, what do you think of? What comes to my mind is crawling across that wide bed, playing, movement, and exploration – maybe pretending to be a slave and the sultan, or the frightened virgin seduced by the pirate of the desert.

IN THE BATHROOM

If you want to transform a room quickly, the bathroom is ideal: turn the light off and just add candles, perfumed oil, bouquets of flowers, and clouds of steam. A beautiful but casual beach hotel in Los Angeles decorates its bathing facilities in the following way: each bathroom possesses a huge window that opens into the bedroom so that you can sit in your swirling jacuzzi and look through both rooms to the picture window on the far side of the bedroom displaying the beach and the sea. The scene in front of you is amazing: it's green and blue and bleached out. It feels like the best kind of holiday.

TRANSFORMING YOUR OWN BATH DECOR

Not everyone has the Pacific Ocean as a backdrop, but who is to say we cannot create our own simulated view? Think seriously about faking a window in the bathroom door by positioning on the door a painting or photograph of:

- the sea (stimulates ideas of lazy summer sexuality)
- the sky (Eastern notions of spiritual sex)
- the tropical rain forest (almost too hot to move, dripping wet as in fevered sex).

ACCESSORIES

Good accessories really make a sensual bathroom. Try little booklets of love poetry dotted around the room, a basket of sweet-smelling nightlights, exotic bathsalts, romantic music, or a handful of fresh crimson rose petals scattered across the swirling green waters of the bathtub.

GODDESS AND
Priest

In this sexual role play, the woman takes the part of the goddess – ready to be worshipped. The man takes the part of the priest – eager to serve. For an entire evening, his job is to give her sexual pleasure and submit to her authority.

You can enact this scenario in any sort of sexual relationship, but it's very useful when the woman finds it difficult to relax and receive sexual pleasure or finds it difficult to talk about sex. It is also good when the man usually controls what happens during sex or wants to give his partner a treat.

THE RULES OF THE SCENARIO
The priest must ask the goddess for her permission before he does anything. The goddess is at liberty to say "yes" or "no" to anything without explaining her reasons. The priest must never

argue or challenge; he should be considerate, deferential, and obedient. His role is to give unconditional companionship, and sensual and sexual pleasure. Her role is simply to focus on her needs and sensations without feelings of guilt or the need to reciprocate. She can make sexual demands at any stage.

ENACTING THE SCENARIO

The goddess and priest scenario can take place at home or in a specially-booked hotel bedroom. The themes are luxury and indulgence, so begin the evening by offering your partner a hot bath scented with a few drops of rose essential oil. Light the bathroom with church candles and offer her a glass of champagne. Offer to pour water over her back and shoulders and wash her hair. Don't get in the bath with her – your role is simply to give pleasure.

Spend the next part of the evening being intimate – cuddle and kiss her – and spend time relaxing and talking. Gradually become more intimate: kiss her neck and stroke her hair. But remember to take your cues from her – read her body language and try to imagine what she would most like you to do. If she responds positively to your kissing, then step up the intimacy. Don't go straight for her genitals though. Concentrate on her upper body; stroke her shoulders and caress her breasts, and ask her if she would like a massage.

GAME ANALYSIS

The reasoning behind this game is that through the priest being forced to ask every single time he wants to do something, the goddess is given a sense of control. Therefore, if she is quite inhibited, she can take the scenario at what feels like a safe pace, because it is her own pace.

When you know that your partner is aroused, ask her if you can undress her. Then give her a sexual

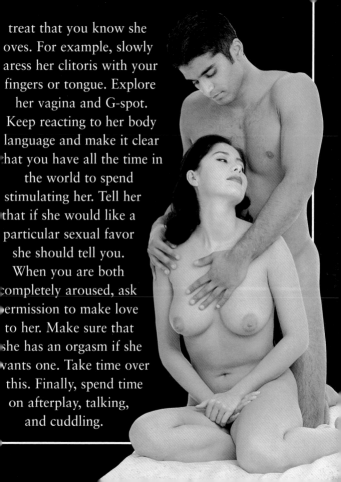

treat that you know she loves. For example, slowly caress her clitoris with your fingers or tongue. Explore her vagina and G-spot. Keep reacting to her body language and make it clear that you have all the time in the world to spend stimulating her. Tell her that if she would like a particular sexual favor she should tell you. When you are both completely aroused, ask permission to make love to her. Make sure that she has an orgasm if she wants one. Take time over this. Finally, spend time on afterplay, talking, and cuddling.

PLAYING WITH
Props

When you move from the sensual world
of massage to that of sex games, the first
thing that you can incorporate into your
love life are certain sensual props and
accessories. If you've never experienced
the teasing of velvet or the slither of silk
across your quivering skin, you now
have a variety of new joys and delights
to anticipate, over the following pages.

SEXY ACCESSORIES FOR
Players

Most of the best sex games use props – items that extend and enhance the action. If straight sex is your favorite, then a vibrator still manages to add to the excitement. If something darker gets your pulse racing, blindfolds, restraints, sex toys, carefully chosen presents, or letters that leave you steaming all extend your experience of sensuality. On the following pages I describe in detail some choice items that you might consider using with your partner to deepen your own shared sexual experience. Begin with the basic but sensual blindfold.

Action tips

- Don't tie a blindfold too tight. You will cut into your partner's eyes, which could be very painful.
- Don't tie a blindfold too loosely. (Unless partial sight is intended as part of a game!)
- The best blindfolds are sleeping masks with elastic bands.

A blindfold offers a sense of helplessness. It lets you feel vulnerable.
You don't know where you are when you wear it. You have no
idea what obstacles you may be facing. Your mind starts racing as
you imagine the hazards that lie outside your ocular range
and your anxiety levels go up and up.

It is these swirling emotions that the astute Games
Master/Mistress picks up on and sagely uses. For
example, most games of restraint include some
version of a soft scarf
tied around the
eyes or a black
velvet eye mask.
It's not just that
the player feels
greater prickles
of sensuality as
he lies there
bound and blind. It is
also that he offers an
appealing sight to you,
the Games Mistress.

SEXUAL
Initiation Rites

All dressed up in leather or rubber and looking for somewhere to go? What about a trip to the Games Academy? Perhaps you would like to qualify as a Games Master/Mistress officially? But if you would, you will have to pass the initiation rites.

TAKE THE TEST
You and your partner can take turns trying the following – the recipient should be blindfolded throughout!
• Identify the odors of sex. You're offered a variety of unusual scents and asked to say which you associate with what aspect of the sex act. These

might include: the scent of massage oil, perspiration from the armpit, the odor of rubber, seminal fluid, and vaginal juices.

• Identify tactile temptations. You are offered a variety of unusual materials and textures to comment on. These might include: silk, satin, fur, feathers, ice, toothpaste, or lubricating jelly.

• Identify the accessories of restraint. You are subjected to the sensation of being lightly spanked (with a hand), caned (with a very lightweight bamboo), paddled with a soft suede cat-o'-nine-tails, or stimulated with a fur mit. The prize for guessing right is an extra spanking.

• Identify the mixture of pleasure and pain. You are subjected to stimulation with ice cubes; then rubbed with deep heat;

Action tip

For men and women particularly susceptible to nipple stimulation, you might like to know that one of the year 2000's bestselling sex toys was the nipple clamp!

Nipple clamps and chain with detachable weights

having your ears softly breathed into, then nibbled; to feeling your neck kissed, licked, and then softly bitten; to having your nipples first sucked, then lightly bitten.

• The Stallion. Your undergarments are parted and your genitals exposed. The final part of the test is to see if you can last long enough during intercourse for your examiner to have an orgasm without doing so yourself.

• If you pass this test, you will be awarded the Prize for Achievement. This consists of telling your partner exactly how you would like to have a climax.

TAKE THE ADVANCED TEST

On another occasion, you may like to play a similar game with your partner. This time, make the situation feel that little bit more vulnerable and daring – ensure that there is no blindfold. You might:

• tie up the initiate with light restraints, using silk cords to secure their hands to the head of the bed

• or handcuff your partner by one hand only to the foot of the bed

• include vaginal penetration with a variety of different sex toys

• or anal penetration with small vibrators or plugs.

To make the test harder, forbid them at constant intervals to experience climax. Threaten them that if they do climax, they will have failed. Which can only mean one thing. They will have to re-take the test on another occasion, until they have performed to your complete satisfaction!

ACCESSORIES

As examiner for the Games Academy you will need:

- squares of satin, silk, velvet
- a fur mitt, feathers, ice, lubricating jelly, or some other sex lubricant
- a paddle, a cane, a cat-o'-nine-tails
- nipple restraints
- silken cords, "safe" handcuffs
- vaginal and anal vibrators and plugs.

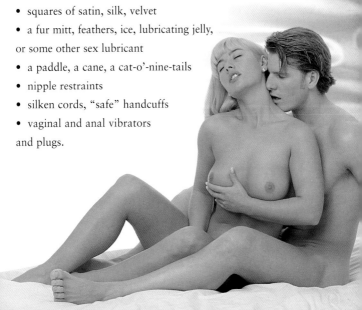

FANTASIES WITH
Blindfolds

Perhaps as a result of their impaired visual ability, blind people often develop a greatly enhanced sense of hearing. Certain noises get easily translated into internal meaning, making their minds capable of racing away to the most dramatic scenarios. Which is why using a blindfold when lovemaking can concentrate the mind wonderfully. For a blindfold game that is based on a long-standing and widely popular sexual fantasy, emulate the great silent screen star Rudolph Valentino, in *The Sheik*:

FOR THE WOMAN

Blindfold your woman and tell her you are taking her into the harem of a Turkish sultan. Since he is extremely ugly, she is not allowed to set eyes on him. Should she even be caught peeping, she will be under sentence of caning. In the harem she will be attended by eunuchs.

62

These eunuchs must prepare her for the sultan. This preparation consists of oiling and anointing her body and then stimulating her genitals so that she is "ready" for the great king. Your job is to play the roles of the eunuchs and the sultan.

FOR THE MAN

Blindfold your man and tell him you are taking him into a harem of exotic females. These women are allowed to use him in any way that they desire. As you ride him you can forbid him to climax. Manipulate his body with your hands to place him in whatever position is appropriate. The more you use him while forbidding him to climax, the more likely he is to disobey you.

FUN WITH
Feathers

One of the most exotic touch temptations to come out of San Francisco in the heady days of the 1970s was the peacock feather massage. Peacock feathers look gorgeous, skim across the skin, and tickle the innocent recipient into wriggling submission. The best scenario of all was when two gorgeous, near-naked young men armed themselves with plumes and put their eager female clients through an hour of touch ecstasy. And there was not even any sex involved! For these games you will need two peacock feathers or alternatively ostrich plumes and talcum powder.

Feathery tips

- Check first that your partner is not allergic to feathers!
- Don't tie knots too tightly.
- Only play tying-up games if you have your partner's consent and use a code word.

SO HERE'S WHAT YOU CAN DO

• Sweep the plume upward on the inside thigh from knees to genitals "accidentally" knocking the genitals as you reach them.

• Sprinkle your partner with talcum powder and use the feathers to sweep it across her body.

• Write "I love you" with the quill over and over again on your partner's naked breasts.

• Tickle every inch of your partner's skin.

• Use this peacock touch as a sensual massage preliminary.

SOFT STROKES
Stroke your partner with a feather to build eroticism and increase arousal.

SENSUAL *Fabrics*

FEASTING THE BODY WITH FABRICS

Equip yourself with squares of silk, velvet, and fur. Using a long strand of velvet, blindfold your partner and lead them into an excessively heated room. Make sure that the room is already scented with perfume or with a burning sweet-smelling incense. As they stand there blindly, tell them that

they now have to submit to anything you choose to do to them. This is the cue to peel their clothes off slowly, and lay them on a couch or a bed covered by a large piece of velvet. Tell them it is imperative that they lie with their legs apart.

HEIGHTEN THEIR ANTICIPATION

Now is the cue to stroke every inch of their skin with each of the sensual fabrics that you have on hand. You can whisk the fabrics across the main part of their body, tickle, and tease them with each material, and finally use the materials for actual massaging. All the time they will be wondering what is going to happen between their legs. You keep them waiting. Finally, repeat the process with their genitals.

Delicious anticipation

The fact that the blindfolded cannot see:

- heightens their anticipation
- makes them feel especially vulnerable
- encourages their fantasies.

THE
Opera Singer

Phone your lover and tell her that she must repor
for her singing lesson at six o'clock sharp at you
place. Don't take "no" for an answer. If she
complains that she can't sing anyway, say that
now she is about to learn.

When she arrives, invite her into the music room
This may be any room in your home, but will
preferably hold at least one musical instrument.
A piano would be best, but if that's not possible,
a recorder or a guitar would do fine.
Explain to her that you are a stern singing maste
You expect her to get your lesson right and, shou.
she make any mistakes, she will be punished. Beg
by asking her to sing a simple song. Anything wil
do – a nursery rhyme, or a popular song. Make i
clear from the outset that you will be a very hard
taskmaster, criticizing even her most basic errors

Make your instructions more difficult as the lesson progresses. (You need her to make a few mistakes!) You can ask her to sing the note you pitch on the tuning fork, sing in time to the rhythm you set up on the metronome, or maybe echo any nonsense sequence of notes you play first.

THE PUNISHMENTS

By way of "punishment" for failure to follow your instructions, you might get her to take her clothes off one by one, make a phone call in the nude, or bend over to be spanked. Alternatively, you could make her continue singing, but now completely naked and bent over forward.

YOUR ACTIONS

As she continues to sing, both exact your punishments and show your satisfaction with her by alternating light spanking with gentle stroking and rubbing of her bottom.

Lubricate her mouth with your finger (to help the "purity" of her notes), lubricate her vagina with your finger (for the same reason), and force her to continue singing while you penetrate her. Intensify your "punishments" by forcing her to continue while you rub her clitoris with your finger or give her oral sex.

HOMEWORK

When your lesson ends, you might present her with a secret cassette recording of her lesson so that she can take it home and see if there is any way in which she might improve her technique.

GAME ANALYSIS

The game depends on your ability to remain in character. Your strictness as teacher will make your lover feel slightly unnerved, even though she knows it is really you. The fact that you actually carry through the punishments in direct proportion to her ability will annoy her. The fact that you insist on continuing – even though she feels silly and uncertain – will intensify her emotions.

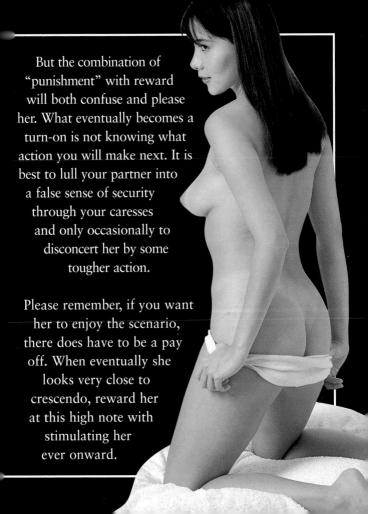

But the combination of "punishment" with reward will both confuse and please her. What eventually becomes a turn-on is not knowing what action you will make next. It is best to lull your partner into a false sense of security through your caresses and only occasionally to disconcert her by some tougher action.

Please remember, if you want her to enjoy the scenario, there does have to be a pay off. When eventually she looks very close to crescendo, reward her at this high note with stimulating her ever onward.

A SEXY
Fur Fantasy

Give your partner a soulful and sexy experience with this Russian-style sex adventure. Tell your story and act it out accordingly. You will need a fur rug or coat for this game.

You are Russian nobles traveling at high speed across the snowy landscape in your *troika*. Wrapped in a fur rug, you are protected from the bitter Russian winter. Suddenly,

the *troika* is brutally halted. Brigands seize you and haul you from the sled. "Strip," they say, and, in the bitter cold, you peel off all your garments. You know you will freeze to death. Then, as the brigands leave, they toss the fur rug toward you, laughing at your nakedness. Wrapping it around you, you stagger toward a wooden hut on the rim of the forest. After you have built a fire there, you eventually fall asleep.

In the morning you wake up to find your partner rubbing the fur across your body and between your legs. Suddenly you are seized around the waist and turned onto your hands and knees. You are taken from the rear. Your partner's hands reach forward and stimulate you from the front. As you sink down in the throes of climax, you hear the whine of the wind across the snowdrifts outside. You know you won't be rescued for days.

PLAYING WITH
Vibrators

In the first of these games, the man is Games Master. In the second game, the woman is Games Mistress. As with all imaginative sex games, the first rule is that you must make absolutely certain your actions will be welcome.

HAPPY UN-BIRTHDAY

"Today," says the Games Master, "is your un-birthday." He produces a beautifully wrapped package. It is your choice whether or not you unwrap it, but if you do, the act of unwrapping means that you agree to fall in with anything he then commands. Since only a serious masochist would NOT

> ## *Action tip*
> For this, or any other scenario to work, you must know that even if there is an impression of other people nearby, there must in actual fact be no possibility of being watched, interrupted, or in any way exposed to the public.

unwrap the parcel, you naturally do so. Inside is a tiny, pencil-slim, ladies' vibrator. "Take off your panties," orders the Games Master. He sits on the sofa and orders you to lie across his knee. He then begins to tickle and stroke your genitals.

Next, the Games Master produces the ladies vibrator, and pleasures your clitoris and labia with the slim vibrating pencil. "Keep your eyes closed at all times now," he commands. As you obediently shut your lids you are pleasurably aware that he has shifted the tiny vibrator from your clitoris to your vagina. Or has he? This vibrator seems to have expanded so that it fills you up. And it twists and whirls inside your vagina in the most extraordinary manner. How can such a tiny vibrator produce such sensation?

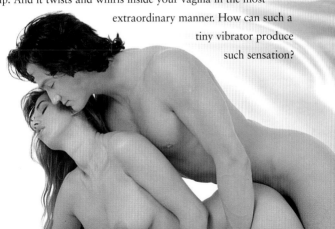

The Games Master's secret? At the stage where you close your eyes he switches the slim pencil vibrator for a larger, dual, vibrator which heightens both your vaginal and clitoral pleasure.

TRYING OUT FOR THE TEAM

The Games Mistress tells you that if you want to play on the team you must try out for it. Clad only in a T-shirt, you are commanded to catch the ball she pitches to you. If you don't catch it, you will be punished. Her throws are impossible to field. Punishment is looming. "Kneel down," she commands. From behind you feel her attach a hard band around the base of your penis and a plastic leash winding from this band between your legs and round the back of your buttocks.

"Answer this question," she commands. The question, when it comes, is impossible. Every time you fail, she switches on a control and the band at the base of your penis vibrates. Eventually, she leaves the vibrating band on full time while simultaneously massaging you by hand. As you climax, you wonder if maybe you actually passed the test after all!

Basic cock ring

Cock ring with anal stimulator

76

Sex toys for girls

There is a huge variety of vibrators available on the market today. Some of these are specially designed for additional clitoral stimulation, or feature imaginative extras.

Dildo

Basic vibrator

Vibrator with clitoral stimulator

Novelty vibrators

Novelty nipple and vaginal vibrator

Ben-wa vaginal balls

Interchangeable heads for vibrators to vary sensations

GETTING INTO
Rubber

You don't have to be a fetishist to admire your lover's appearance when he or she dresses up in shiny black rubber. And did you ever stop to think what it feels like to wear rubber?

It clings to every pore of your skin, grasps and squeezes your flesh, slips, and slides as you exude your sweet-smelling body odor inside its tight confines. The heat that your body generates, trapped inside this sensual coating, raises temperatures in more ways than one. Rubber lovers report feeling so feverish, they fall upon each other with passion.

DOMINATION
Rubber clothes are a great prop for playing sensual domination games.

78

DRESSING GAME

- Dress for a date in close-fitting black latex. Tall black boots are a MUST. Without giving your partner any warning in advance, arrive at your meeting place, clad accordingly. You will look great.
- Back in your apartment, hand your partner a bottle of special oil and ask him/her to rub it in – to your outfit!
- When it comes to taking the outfit off, make sure that your underwear (also rubber) is the specialist sort that allows for lovemaking without removal.
- Hand your partner the bottle of oil and ask him/her to rub it into the naked parts that are now exposed.
- Then rub him/her with oil and slip and slide back and forth all over each other.

79

DRESSING UP IN
Leather

Wet-look leather offers all the appeal that plastic food wrap does and more. Leather is also a recognized fashion material, and shows for leather lovers are a regular part of the fashion season.

GAMES

• Hold your own fashion show. When your partner buys, force them to pay in kind.

• Dress up in leather for sex. Put on fetish underwear, and insist that your partner does likewise before you agree to sex.

Buying leather

City boutiques sell rubber and leather clothes and accessories, as do mail order companies and internet websites.
See the appendix.

GETTING ALL
Wrapped Up

Plastic food wrap may not have been your first choice of sex toy, but it can be subtly provocative and surprisingly erotic when used in imaginative ways. You could try:

• winding your partner's torso in such a way as to make her breasts jut out from the wrapping, with the nipples tightly encased in the plastic

• winding between your partner's legs so that her labia are trapped open under a layer of plastic food wrap that does not obstruct the entrance to the vagina. Or around his scrotum to form a kind of testes ring, or around the shaft of his penis with only the head left free.

WARNING!
Never put plastic food wrap on or near your partner's face. This could be extremely dangerous.

81

CREATING A
Bond

A Games Master understands that for many
men and women, helplessness is a precursor of
sexual arousal. It is also a sex enhancer, since the
state of mind the bonds evoke means that you
experience the sex act with increased sexual sensitivity.

THE PRISONER GAME

Forbid the prisoner to make any move herself. Undress her,
linger over her breasts and genitals, and "interfere" with her.
Tell her that as a criminal she must be punished.

EQUIPMENT

You will need some lengths of light chain or silk ties. Ideally,
the prisoner will have pierced nipples and nipple rings. If she
possesses nipple rings, slip the chain or ties through these, take
it to her thigh and secure it so that it will be difficult for her to
move very far without the chain or silk
tie pulling on her breast.

TORTURE THE PRISONER

Your torture might consist of:

• wrapping the chains around her breasts and tweaking her nipples, or briefly slipping on a pair of nipple clamps and vibrating these. (You can now buy vibrating nipple clamps)

• wrapping the chains between her buttocks and slipping them between the folds of her vagina then masturbating her like this

• treating her body like a table and eating off her

• telling her to kneel on all fours and, as you masturbate her, order her to keep completely still. If she moves, you will stop your action

• moving the chains to each side of her inner thighs and riding her yourself.

COMFORT
*If you bind her, ensure
that she is comfortable.*

AT HIS
Expense

There is a swathe of people who feel extremely powerful in their everyday life and who are bathed in self-confidence. Yet it is these people who need to be taken to extremes in order to feel so small that they can relax, putting themselves totally in the versatile hands of the Games Master/Mistress.

THE SELF-ABASEMENT GAME

This is a game based on teasing and works well with powerful men who respond erotically to humiliation.

• Persuade your man to be tied up. If he complains, tell him you will promise him anything he likes afterwards.

• When he is strapped up in as provocative a manner as possible (you might wind the ties around his genitals), tell him: "So you thought you were going to get all kinds of sexual favors for agreeing to this. You poor fool. You really fell for it, didn't you? What a stupid man you are!"

84

• Now describe his needs to him and tell him how pathetic they are. Explain to him that you know he would like to do X, Y, and Z. Then sneer at these ideas.

• Stand in front of him and masturbate, just close enough so that he can almost touch you – but not quite…! "I'd bet you'd like to do this," you might say, as you continue with your self-stimulation. "Oh, that feels good."

• If even more self-abasement is what he craves, lead him around like a dog, ride him like a horse, and joke about his bizarre needs as you do so.

• Finally, give him a pay-off by stimulating his genitals, telling him as you do so that he has absolutely no choice but to take whatever interference you choose to deal out to him.

Safeguard

Assess your partner carefully before trying out verbal domination. With the wrong partner, this game could be distressing.

THE BIG
Stick

Caning and spanking may sound
like painful experiences to some, but
to many people a light slip of the
hand or a playful blow with a carpet
beater brings the blood pleasantly to the
surface, tingling, and warming the skin – all
precursors of erotic arousal. This degree of
spanking or caning stings, but it does not hurt.
If your partner's administrations begin to cause
pain, call a halt. Pretend pain is one thing, real
torture is totally unacceptable.

TORTURE PROPS
*Domination clothing
and props will
enhance caning.*

SAFE INSTRUMENTS

Carpet beaters, paddles, spatulas, whisks, and soft flails do NOT hurt. Crops, rulers, and canes DO hurt, so only use them sparingly.

GAME – WHERE WOULD YOU LIKE IT?

• In this game you offer your partner light spanking or caning – whichever will be most acceptable.

• You ask "Where would you like it? Here or there?" When your partner says "Here," then spank or cane somewhere else.

• When your partner protests, then do it somewhere else again. The idea is to tease and tantalize.

Of course, sometimes you will spank in the desired place. But the aim is to frustrate your partner as much as to satisfy them. But why frustrate your partner? Because it rouses people. And any arousal increases sexual turn-on.

Action tip

Don't forget to agree on a safety code word first.

A BINDING
Agreement

Spanking games are not just about providing the recipient with pleasurable pain. Played carefully, they are also humorous episodes, since they depend on the conundrum of the "bind" and the "double bind." These double binds can be produced by arranging the game in such a way that the player cannot win, whatever they do. For example, you establish rules at the beginning – but then, as you play the game, you suddenly change those rules without warning. You impose new

thresholds. You deliberately arrange the play so that somehow your partner never gets it quite right.

THE "THANK YOU" GAME

Every time you paddle your lover, he must say "thank you."

PADDLES
Use a leather sex paddle and wear an eye mask for this enjoyable spanking game.

• If he forgets because he's carried away by the eroticism of the stroke, he must be penalized with another stroke.

• If he doesn't sound enthusiastic enough, paddle harder.

• If he sounds too enthusiastic, accuse him of over-doing it.

• Make him count the strokes, but then insist that he's got it wrong – even (or especially) when he hasn't.

SAFETY PRECAUTIONS

Work out what your partner wants to take in the way of punishment. Do not impose your own ideas. If you are spanking, remove all rings from your fingers first. If you are tempted to cane lightly, try the instrument out on your own hand first! And when you know just how much of a sting it provides, think carefully before administering blows to your partner.

BONDAGE
Slave Game

The room is dark. A single candle burns in a corner. You lead your slave into the room and order her to take off all her clothes. There is a black sheet draped across the bed. The bed must either be made of metal or be a four-poster bed, so that there is somewhere you can tie your slave up to.

PUNISHING THE BAD SLAVE

Your partner has been a bad slave, and you explain to her that bad slaves must always be punished for their wrongdoing. Order her to kneel against the bed. When she does so, tie her hands with soft ties (men's neckties serve well for this purpose), securing one to each side of the bed. Pull her arms forward as you tie her wrists, so that her naked rear

90

is exposed and her genitals are fully in view. This will make her feel more helpless and at the mercy of your desires.

Then you leave the room. Just when she thinks you have forgotten about her, you re-enter. And discover that she has moved slightly. This is totally forbidden, you tell her, and so she must be punished. She protests, but unsuccessfully. You might punish her by rubbing her bottom first so that it gets warm and then spanking it lightly to give her a shock. Each time you come back into the room you discover she has moved, and the punishment continues. You might lightly cane her, or maybe pretend to rape her.

LOVING WITH
Mirrors

Mirrors, placed at strategic points in your room of love, can be used for special games of exhibitionism and voyeurism, and always add a certain frisson to sexual proceedings.

MIRROR GAMES

• You might pretend that the mirror is a window into the room next door. In that room are two lovers who are performing specially for you.

• You might angle your lovemaking so that you can actually

Anatomy lessons

You might play at anatomy lessons by having your lover expose certain areas of your genitals, such as the clitoris or the rim of the anus, then for him to demonstrate, for your education, just what happens when these are specifically stimulated. As the pupil, you are compelled to watch the demonstration model in the looking glass.

see the penis moving in and out of the vagina so that the mirror becomes a kind of porno movie. You might position yourself right in front of the mirror so that watching yourself becomes part of a game of submission and domination.

• One of you might order the other to do something specifically sexual that they may never have viewed before. This might be the act of fellatio or cunnilingus, or having sex on a chair in front of the mirror.

• Your lover might tell you that it is your job to turn them on. You could do this by stimulating yourself while your partner is reflected watching you.

• Your lover might assist you by masturbating himself as he becomes increasingly aroused by your reflected activities.

LISTEN TO
My Tape

Total trust is necessary here, because one of you has to agree to obey the other – any game where you put yourself completely into someone else's power is not to be carried out with strangers or with anyone with whom you feel uncertain.

Arrange to meet at a borrowed apartment and be there first to welcome your partner lovingly when she arrives. Ask her to undress and lie down on the bed. Then tie her arms and legs securely yet softly with silken ties. Last of all, gently tie a soft blindfold around her head.

Once she is settled, promise her that great things will happen. Give her a loving kiss and leave the room. Leave her for 15 minutes – just long enough for her to start getting restless and to wonder what is happening, but not long enough to get angry.

When she demands attention, it's your cue to say: "Well, I can't attend to you right now – you'd better make do with this," and put a small personal stereo down next to her.

Inside it is a cassette tape, on one whole side of which you have recorded yourself saying the most suggestive, lecherous, and arousing things you can think of and outlining what marvellous plans you have for lovemaking with her.

THE SURPRISE

What she doesn't know, but is going to find out, is how long the recording continues. This isn't a five-minute tape – it goes on and on, for 45 minutes.

She, lying on that bed, is unable to move, incapable of escaping the voice, or the blindfold, or the silken knots, however much she wants to. And if she is responsive to your suggestions, she will be desperate to do something about them. When you finally return, she's going to be as angry as she is erotically inflamed.

YOU NEED TOTAL TRUST

This is your cue to ask her what she would like to happen next. Her answer is most likely to be "Untie me immediately and take the blindfold off!" You may reply, "OK, but when I've released you, I am going to subject you to all kinds of indignities and you will have to accept them. If you don't agree, there will be no untying." Your "indignities" will consist of a wonderful erotic massage, performed when she is unbound but reblindfolded.

THE PLEASURE

After massaging her body, tell her that you have to leave the room again briefly but you are not going to retie her. You're putting her on trust not to move away from the bed.

While you are out of the room, quickly change your clothes, put on an unfamiliar aftershave, then don very thin surgical gloves and coat them with massage oil. When you return, give her a genital massage but without saying a word. Since she is still unable to see you, it is quite possible that she will think you are someone else.

REASSURE HER

When she actually has her orgasm, at last take off the blindfold and hold her close to you. Tell her that you love her, and reassure her that there was nobody else in the room at any point in the game. Ask her if she enjoyed the experience.

DOCTORS AND *Nurses*

If the Games Master decrees that you play "Doctors and Nurses" (no actual uniforms required), and keep in character, it can become surprisingly sexy.

THE GAME

Decide which of you is to be the doctor and which the nurse. If you want to don a white coat (as the doctor), then feel free. But don't bother if this isn't really your scene. When you are properly in character, ask your patient to hop up on to a table (suitably padded), having first removed their underwear.

If the patient is female, ask her to spread her legs wide open and then insert a surgically gloved finger into her vagina and press on different areas around the entrance. Be gentle as you do this, but maintain the professional air of the doctor.

Ask your "patient" to comment on the different degrees of sensation she is experiencing when you practice these different moves on her. Next, ask her to get on her hands and knees so that you can do an inspection from the rear. Using separate surgical gloves examine her anal opening and, again, ask her to rate the different sites for sensation.

If the patient is male, put on surgical gloves, hold his penis and inspect it closely. If he has a foreskin, slide it down and measure the penis size. Slide your finger around the head and across the top of his penis. Hold and measure the weight of his testicles and stroke down the connection between testicles and base of penis.

DRESS TO KILL
Turn him on with sexy outfits and erotic props.

PLAYING
Strip Poker

Everyone knows the old-fashioned way of
playing this card game. For every loss during
the game, you remove an item of clothing. If
you are playing with a bunch of friends,
this can be a daring experiment. But what
about a private game between two lovers?
Couldn't we dream up something a little more intimate?
Here's a sexier version of the game for only two players.

THE GAME

The Games Master deals five cards each. On the strength of
this first deal, you both place a bet.

Value of the cards – highest through to lowest:
- Royal Flush – Ace, King, Queen, Jack and Ten
- Straight Flush – five cards of the same suit in a running suit.
For example, 9, 8, 7, 6, 5
- Flush – five cards, of any suit, but in order

- Full House – three of one number and two of another, for example, three 8s and two 6s
- A Triple – three of a kind and two unconnected cards
- Pairs – two pairs, for example, two 2s and two 3s and one unconnected card
- One pair – plus three unconnected cards
- Highest of a bad hand. No runs, no pairs – just the highest card of all.

At the next deal you can throw in any poor cards and have new ones substituted. You bet again. The betting continues until one of you calls a halt. The last to bet shows their hand. The winner scoops the pot. The loser has to obey the winner's instructions.

TAKING POSSESSION OF THE WINNINGS

The winner subjects the loser to sexual forfeits. To make the game more interesting, you might start with lighter sorts of touch, carried out on the less sexually significant parts of the body. From there on the winner cashes in their stakes by subjecting the loser to increasingly blatant sexual forfeits!

These forfeits might consist of:

- taking a top and (if female) a bra off
- massaging, rubbing, and stroking the breasts
- massaging, rubbing, and sucking the nipples (yes, men too)
- removing clothing on the lower half
- subjecting the loser's genitals to any number of graduated stimulations from stroking, through to oral sex, or using a vibrator

• subjecting the loser to intercourse
but for a few minutes only.
The stop-start stimulation
that the loser will experience
with this method is maddening
and provocative. It heightens both
arousal and impatience.

REMINDER

Don't forget that people often feel more
vulnerable when only a few of their clothes have been removed
than if all have been cast to the winds. If your partner is shy,
reassure them that the slow process of removing their clothes is
all part of a heightening of sexual tension that can lead to
incredible lovemaking.

Action tip

The opportunities for bluffing give the game an increased
element of daring and risk. If you are found out you know
you will have to pay a penalty, so the element of anticipation
heightens the proceedings.

IF MUSIC BE THE
Food of Love

The impact of sex is heightened by anything that plants suggestion inside the heads of the players. One of the tasks of the Games Master, therefore, must be to arrange not just the decor of the Love Rooms but also the small details – the little things that heighten the atmosphere. Music is a vital part of the ambience of any sexual situation, be it to aid straightforward lovemaking or to suggest something more programmed.

Fascinating fact

Recent neurological research has shown that Baroque music resembles the pattern of certain brain sequences that fire into life during learning. When certain works by Mozart are played, it has been proved that learning is subsequently improved. It doesn't take much of a leap to see that music might have a similar impact on the experience of sex. It's just a question of going through your CD collection and finding out what fits your particular tricky mind!

Most people know about the impact of the golden oldies when they are played at full blast in the bedroom. The best sounds of Frank Sinatra, Dean Martin, and Ella Fitzgerald have been wowing men and women for half a century. And they are great – no doubt about that – if romance is what you are looking for. But suppose your taste is Gothic? Or darker still? Suppose what you've always longed for is to be swept away by animal passion? Or you wish to float up to heaven on a cloud of ecstatic sexual purity? The right music is the key.

Here are my suggestions:

• Rachmaninov's Second and Third Piano Concertos – excellent for passion

• *Dido's Lament* from *Dido and Aeneus* by Purcell, sung by Jessye Norman – for ecstatic purity

• Leonard Cohen's *Jazz Police* and *I'm Your Man* – from the CD entitled *I'm Your Man* – for definitely darker tastes.

SEXY SNAPSHOTS AND
Photographs

The sophisticated Games Master or Mistress knows that a camera can capture certain erotic moments. If you want to recollect your naked man standing half in shadow, looking at you with unashamed desire, the next best thing to reality is to keep his celluloid alter ego in your wallet.

One woman sent her man a series of gorgeous snapshots (shot with a remote camera mechanism) where she posed as:

- an old-fashioned Edwardian pin-up in full period costume
  - a dominatrix complete with thigh-high shiny boots and a whip
  - a dish at a banquet
  - a sultry houri.

THE SNAPSHOTS

Work out the idea that you want to transmit. If the imagination counts for a

106

lot with you, you won't be pleased with a full frontal view, where one of you is stimulating yourself directly to the camera. An image like this leaves nothing to the imagination. The right way is to set the camera on automatic, then pose, with your partner, in an extremely compromising position, behind the clouded glass shower door. You won't be able to see everything in the resulting picture. But you'll offer some very tempting glimpses.

On the other hand, a lot of guys adore the full-frontal look so, first rule of the game, assess your partner's personal tastes!

The risks

The advantage of digital cameras is that the pictures will not have to be processed at the photo lab. The disadvantage is that you might find compromising shots of yourself beamed around the planet by email via the internet.

WRITING
Love Notes

The whole point of a love note is to remind the other person of your existence and to show them that you care. The best way to do this is to catch their attention with something that excites, intrigues, or stimulates them. You might manage this by making them laugh, wonder, or by directly turning them on.

GAMES

• Leave a note tucked under the windshield wiper on your partner's car that says "Nice car. How about a rally?"

• Send an invitation that says "Esmeralda Diamond invites you to a banquet. Main course – Esmeralda Diamond."

• Send half a photograph – the top half – accompanied by a note that says, "if you would like information on how to acquire the other half, meet me at such and such."

• Write a note in the shape of a Classified Ad saying "Young hooker needs rescuing. If you think you might be able to prevent me from walking the streets, please meet me at Jimmy's gay bar."

Follow this up by dressing the part and waiting at a bar possessing some kind of a sexual reputation. It is important always to fulfill any sexual or other promise that you might make in a love note.

• Or if you are a man: "Young transvestite urgently seeks moral reformer. Meet me at Madame Fifi's." Dress up in full drag, and remember, don't forget the eye shadow. Act the part and, who knows, you might give your partner a real thrill.

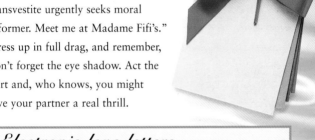

Electronic love letters

Did you know that there are whole sites on the Internet geared towards communicating a little eroticism into your lover's life? For example, *www-kinkycards.com* will send your partner, completely free of charge, a romantic note, an old Edwardian pin-up picture, or a no-holds-barred kinky card. And there are certain art sites that offer very beautiful works of erotic art, copies of which can be downloaded.

DREAMING UP
Sexy Gifts

As with all suggestions in this book, you need to assess your partner's individual likes and dislikes. That way, you won't pitch presents and love notes inappropriately. Sending a pair of soiled underpants to a guy a day after you've first met him will certainly make an impact, but it may not be entirely the one you are looking for. Giving a sensitive girl a transparent purple vibrator gift-wrapped in shiny paper – when the most she was hoping for was Valentine chocolates – will probably inspire her to run a mile in four minutes.

At the very beginning of love, give:

- sentimental cards
- interesting books
- flowers
- chocolates.

When the friendship is heating up, give:

- silk boxers
- sexy books
- suggestive cards
- erotic pictures.

When the friendship is boiling, give:

- champagne
- chocolate body paint (you lick it off)
- genital lubricant with a note saying "I'm longing to rub this between your legs"
- crotchless panties
- nipple clamps.

When the friendship is off the wall:

- a giant double dildo
- one of the new sex lubricants (You pop a capsule into your mouth and break it with your teeth during oral sex so that your lover is bathed in sweet-smelling gel. It's also edible.)

MAKING A
Sex Tape

Those of us who are new-technology freaks love the idea of their own sound recording studio. At a very basic level, just collecting and downloading your favorite tunes can be a starting point for those oh-so-sexy nights in. And if you've read the previous pages on the erotic power of sound, you'll know what I'm talking about.

The dedicated Games Master/Mistress goes one step further, however. The seduction of music is one thing, but the power of your own voice is quite another. You can tape-record all kinds of sexy blandishments. These might run from giving your girlfriend a frisson as she plugs in her radio on the way to work, all the way through to thrilling her, when she's lonely without you one night, with a sexy reading of an unusually erotic short story that she can listen to in the privacy of her own gothic four-poster bed. If you are in need of a story, take a look at the end of this book for inspiration.

TAPE TALES

You might record:

- erotic short stories
- S and M commands
- an endless list of sexual praise
- commands or conversation between *two* voices, so that your partner gets the idea that there are two of you in the room.

A CHANGE OF
Scene

Change is important in all aspects of life,
and sex is no exception. We all need
variety and a change of pace. However
much you adore your gorgeous partner,
human nature dictates that you will
enjoy sexuality more if you try different
things. If you occasionally change only
one item in your sexual pattern, your
sexual batteries will be recharged.

WHY DO WE NEED *Change?*

By taking the step of buying this book, you have set change in motion. Even contemplating an alteration in your experience of sex means that you have instigated a new movement in your brain. Sex games are, by their very nature, novel. They are also forms of play. And that's what is so great about being an adult human being. Sex allows you to go back to the days of play, which you probably last enjoyed as a child.

Novelty comes in many shapes and forms. If, occasionally, you inject something different into your sexual experience, the whole of your sex life becomes enhanced.

SEX EVOLUTION

We need change in order to remain flexible; we need change in order to develop as human beings, and we need change so that we can keep pace with an ever-moving world. Our sex lives are no exception to this basic rule of living.

New patterns of life probably mean new patterns of lovemaking. Perhaps in another hundred years when we have colonized the asteroid belt, we will experience sex as flying, since we may be doing it in conditions where there is no gravity. Telephone sex is a recent example of sexual change in the present day.

A thought for the future – in only a very short time, you will also be able to have sex via the internet through visual contact, thanks to personalized web-TV. The future of sex is here.

TELEPHONE
Sex

Anyone can dial into a sex chat line and be talked through self-stimulation. There's nothing very special about this. But when you are talking erotica down the line with someone you know and like and who really turns you on, that is a whole different ball game!

THE RULES

- Give yourself lots of time when you won't be interrupted.
- Make your own circumstances as pleasant as possible. Warmth, candlelight, or perfume in the air, are all delicious ingredients.

- Sit or lie somewhere comfortable and private.
- Make sure that anything you might want during sex is within arm's reach.

THE ACTION

- Be truthful. Tell it like you are really feeling it.
- Don't fake anything.
- If you are missing your partner, let them know this. If there are things that you wish they were doing to you, voice them as clearly and as graphically as possible.
- If there are things you know they would like to have done to them, let them know how you would carry out these actions if you happened to be on the spot.
- Talk about self-stimulation. Talk your partner through what you are doing and what they are doing. If you use a vibrator, do so letting your man know that in your imagination he is holding this sex toy and rubbing it around your clitoris and vagina. If you are applying lubricant to yourself as you speak, let your woman know that in your head this feels as if she were applying it to you. Her hand is on your penis. Your massage oils are her very own, sweet-smelling love juices. This is how eloquent you want to be.

SEX ON THE
Net

The internet offers the next big leap in our love lives. However, although it is very possible to achieve an extraordinary degree of intimacy with friendships made through chat rooms and instant message services, no one would deny that as long as you have your hands on a keyboard, it's hard to actually have sex, with yourself or with anyone else. But that is due to change, and quite soon. The next development will be the

widespread availability of personalized web cameras – tiny little cameras perched on top of your computer. This means that interactive film sex will be possible, with instant visual communication, even if you are thousands of miles apart.

THE RULES

• Make the physical circumstances around you as visually erotic as possible.

• Be natural with your interactive partner. If you are shy or nervous, don't be afraid to say so. In spite of the cameras, you need to remember that this is not a performance, it is the making of a sexual relationship, and these only work effectively if you can truly "let go" of yourself.

• Follow the action lines for telephone sex (see pages 118–19).

Photography should always be fun and photographic content on the Net is no exception. If you enjoy yourself, it will show in the picture you transmit and you will appear all the sexier for it. So relax, then take time while pleasuring yourself to the erotic accompaniment of your lover's interactive appreciation.

Paid arousal

Of course there are people who provide web camera sex services already. But these are NOT personalized services. They are acts done to an impersonal camera. They may be arousing, but they remain firmly in the category of sex for pay.

ADVENTURES IN
the Woods

Some people like to play games in the imagination only. Others get a huge kick out of experiencing the real thing. Years ago, I met a man who called himself "The Fixer." This man claimed to be able to make other people's fantasies come true.

One of his woman friends, he said, had longed to be tied to a tree in a public place and forced to submit to the sexual attentions of any passing male. The Fixer had, he said, set up this dream, only he chose a part of a public forest that was little frequented, and the two men who did "stroll by and take advantage" were sent there by him and were not strangers.

This took place in the 1970s. Today, nobody in their right mind would indulge in any casual unprotected sex, and even if multiple sex partners have been arranged by a friend, there is still a health risk involved. But you can set up something similar, using blindfolds, disguises, and varied sexual actions to appear to be a whole variety of different individuals.

Safety measures

Sex in the open air can be a
very happy experience, not
to mention an earthy one.
But it's also important to
remember that there are
laws about committing a
public nuisance, so it is
important only to
make love where you
definitely cannot be
observed. Otherwise you
might find yourself in deep
trouble with the authorities.

ROOM
Mates

The word "room" has two meanings. One is "chamber" or
"apartment," the other is "space." This is an important
distinction in a sexual context, since lovemaking in the same
room may be comfortable, but after a while it can also become
very dull. It's as if the sexual psyche occasionally needs extra
space in order to stretch and expand.

Earlier on, I discussed the concept of a "love
room" instead of just a "bedroom." But here the
idea is to move out and broaden your ideas
about good places in which to feel erotic.

SEX AT HOME

If you are fortunate enough to enjoy guaranteed
privacy, then sex in the living room on a sheepskin rug
in front of a roaring log fire need not be just a
Christmas fantasy: it can actually take place and
feel great anytime. Maybe it feels so good

because it takes us back to that plain old novelty factor – because it is different, it feels different.

GAME

Settle down to a comfortable evening in the living room in front of the television, making sure that the room is well heated – in fact, overheated. Put on a video. But surprise your partner with a really sexy one such as 9½ *Weeks*. As the action in the film heats up, begin caressing your lover, casually, but as if you can't help yourself. Thanks to the heat, you have the perfect excuse to shed a few garments as things progress, and if you don't fall on each other during the film action, there's every likelihood you will do so during the credits.

125

SEX IN THE
Office

Of course we shouldn't do it. The risk of a colleague finding out is very great, even if you have closed and locked the door of the office. And if this does happen, you're in trouble. Yet many of us brave the possible complications for incredible erotic experiences.

THE RISK FACTOR

There's a real risk, in that you may get discovered. But there is also an imagined risk, in that while you are actually having sex you are aware that discovery is a possibility. The imagined risk is what heightens the experience, actually raising adrenaline levels and giving an added natural chemical boost to the proceedings!

GAME

• Make sure the office door is locked and the telephone off the hook, but try to do this without letting your partner know.

126

- Tell your partner you are expecting an imminent visit from a senior colleague.
  - Tell your partner that you are incredibly turned on by them and simply can't wait a moment longer. You must have sex with them *now*.
    - As you tell them this, begin caressing and stimulating them.
    - Tell them that you are sure your meeting won't take place for at least five minutes.
  - Have sex.

Danger point

There is a chance that your lover will be so anxious about the situation that their reaction may be negative rather than aroused. Try to judge your partner's emotions accurately in advance: ensure that they are turned on rather than scared.

SUNTAN

Wrestling

Invite your friend over to take part in some sports games. Meet them at the front door wearing a mask. As they enter your home, show them into a side room and hand them a "costume." Ask them to change into it so that they are ready for the proceedings. The costume should consist of a skimpy bikini if they are female, a pair of skimpy briefs if they are male, and a mask.

When your partner has changed, invite them into the "sports arena." This is your living room with the furniture put to one side and thick towels laid down on top of a plastic underlay. (Garbage bags or a huge shower curtain will work well.) Stand your partner in the middle of the room and coat them liberally with suntan oil. Ask them to coat you liberally, too. Explain that the object of the

game is to get the best of three falls, but that if one of you (usually the man) has a height or weight advantage, they must be handicapped. The best way to do this is probably to strap one arm behind their back. The wrestling consists of a good deal of slithering about. As an added bonus you should definitely do your best to remove their costume during the activities.

Action tip

Don't take the idea of falls too seriously. The most fun in this game is to be had out of slithering around each other's near-naked bodies with snakelike sensuousness.

129

INSIDE THE
Small Hotel

Moving into a discreet hotel for an afternoon or evening can allow all kinds of unspoken fantasies to spring into reality. Here is one story of what happened when a young woman acted out something she had only ever previously read about.

"I knew stories about hookers turning up at their clients' apartments wearing little or nothing under their coats, and I often wondered at their daring. Then, one night, my lover had to stay in a hotel near where I lived because he was attending a conference there. He invited me to visit him, so I took a deep breath and took off most of my clothes, retaining only my flimsy underwear and stockings covered by my great-aunt's old fur coat."

"Just walking from the car to the hotel entrance filled me full of adrenaline. And once inside, I was

terrified that the receptionist would
think I was a hooker and would
throw me out. To make matters
worse, the fur coat wouldn't close
and I was aware that if I didn't hold
it very firmly drawn together, it might
gape open and everyone in the lobby
would see that I was naked. Just the
thought of this possibility made me
go hot and cold all over. To my relief,
if the receptionist thought there was
anything strange going on, he didn't show it.

The walk to the hotel room seemed to take forever.
I had to wait at an elevator and got jostled when a
bunch of young men tumbled out of it. Then the
hotel corridors all looked the same and I walked
down the wrong one and panicked because I
thought I wasn't going to find my lover. He had no
idea I was going to try this experiment, so when he
opened the door to his room, I just tweaked the
lapel of the coat open for a minute and then

tweaked it back quickly so that no one else would see. He understood immediately.

"He drew me inside and laid me down on the huge hotel bed. He wouldn't let me take the coat off and actually held the top half closed while he parted the bottom half with his other hand. He didn't say anything much either, which was fantastically sexy. It was as if he was playing out the fantasy. I was a hooker, I'd arrived in his room and he was making use of me. I was so nervous I was on fire already and I climaxed almost as soon as he came inside me. The physical thrill of actually living something I'd fantasized about was incredible."

SAFETY TIP

Please be aware that acting out a fantasy means it may lose its excitement if it becomes routine – indulge in this kind of action sparingly, so that your imagination can retain its special catalog of sex tales.

IN YOUR
Automobile

BACK SEAT DRIVING

Drive out to the nearest secluded spot and tell your lover that you are going to set a challenge. With one of you in the back seat and the other in the front, the back seat lover has got to bring the front seat lover to orgasm. You think it's impossible? Well, give it a try... It's not! Just be sure that you select a parking place that is genuinely secluded and private.

MAKING OUT

It's back to the 1940s for this sex game. You, your lover, and another couple drive off, preferably to a drive-in movie. Halfway through the film you "make out." Some people might interpret this to mean "going all the way," others might just see this as an opportunity for "heavy petting." It's up to you. The idea is to preserve the classic atmosphere of the 1940s. Right down to the popcorn.

ON YOUR
Bike

LADY GODIVA

Motorcycles and black leather are one sexy combination. In the Lady Godiva game, the lady biker, clad in a skirt and no panties, sits astride your shiny machine as you race around town.

A POWERFUL THROTTLE

This is one to try in the garage with the doors firmly closed. Sit on the bike facing each other, start the engine, and see if you can manage to have sex in time to the vibrations of the motorcycle. Or just try it doggy-style over the bike's saddle....

> ### *Caution*
> Make sure there is always **adequate ventilation** in the garage to avoid any noxious fumes.

SEX GAMES FOR THE
Spring

Celebrate the beginning of the new season with a change. Take
your beloved partner away for a weekend treat. Stay at a nice
country-style hotel or, if you can't afford this, borrow a friend's
apartment somewhere. After an early supper, retire to the
bedroom and inform your partner that you are going to
celebrate the Spring Solstice.

- Give each other a warm bath.
- Lay your partner down on the bed.
- Decorate them with spring flowers.
- Give each other gifts.

SEX GAMES FOR THE
Summer

Summer on the patio, roasting beneath the sun's rays while resting on a sun lounger. Did you know that if the sun beams between your legs for long enough it can turn you on? When you decide it's time to start avoiding sunburn, propose that you both retreat indoors for a cool drink. Wait on your partner with an exotic cocktail (you can buy them pre-mixed in the supermarket), wearing a white napkin over your arm as you deliver, and, when they have drunk it, explain that now they must pay the bill – in kind. If there are complaints, insist that this is a fair exchange, and don't take no for an answer.

SEX GAMES FOR THE
Fall

Fall is harvest time. Tell your lover that you are going to hold a Fruit Fest. Invite them over to view your gorgeously decorated room, with exotic fruit heaped around it. Tempt them with some iced grapes, while offering them champagne in a fluted glass. As they get more into the mood, decorate them with grapes and peaches and mushy fruits such as strawberries. Or, if you feel really confident that they will understand the workings of your mind, decorate yourself as if you were the exhibit at a Harvest Festival. Then don't hesitate to celebrate by eating the fruit and each other.

SEX GAMES FOR THE
Winter

Want to relieve the gloom of those dark cold days? Think candlepower. Set up dozens of candles in the bedroom. Use no other lighting. Inform your co-games-player that the time has come to drive out the spirits of winter and call on the sun to reappear and bring its heat. Dress yourself and your partner in a long, full robe (preferably white), turn the lights off all over the house and, with each of you carrying a white candle, step slowly to the bedroom, chanting as you go along. Decree that your partner must be the vessel through which you will try to reach the sun. Now subject them to a number of sexual moves, so that both they and the bedroom become red hot and your incantation therefore appears to have worked!

GETTING
Wet

Water is a gorgeous, inspirational, sensual aphrodisiac. Sex in the bath can be achingly funny, and lovemaking in the shower is slippery, and slidy, steamy, and very hot indeed! Natural settings, such as waterfalls and lapping waves, are every woman's ideal and inspire the floating male to some very eellike writhing indeed.

AQUATIC
Love Fun

FOREPLAY AND AFTERPLAY IN THE TUB

Foreplay in the bath is fun and, even if your bath
isn't big enough to have sex in, you can
make love sitting on the edge of the tub
or on the bathroom floor, should your
gleaming naked body prove inspirational
to your appreciative partner.
Bathing before sex makes you
feel clean and confident; bathing
after sex enhances relaxation
and intimacy.

SEX IN WATER

Water is a supportive
medium: your body
becomes weightless
and you can move

around freely, which means you can swim into sex positions that ordinarily would mean some unlikely contortion. The best time many of us will find for free-floating sensuality is late at night, in the dark, in the warm sea, when no-one can see you.

HYDROTHERAPY

Hydrotherapy uses water to stimulate and heal the body. The therapeutic jets come in the form of baths, showers, whirlpools, steam rooms, saunas, and sea water treatments. Jacuzzis alone have brought a whole new dimension to love. Being pounded by streams of water on one side and your flushed and excited partner on the other is the stuff that holidays are made of.

Sex tips

If you are feeling tired and sluggish, and you want to energize yourself before sex, spend 15 minutes soaking in a hot bath and then stand up and take a quick cold shower. Your pores will close rapidly and will leave you feeling invigorated. If you are totally stressed out, a warm bath relaxes you enough to bring on lazy feelings of sensuality.

SHOWER
Power

The shower is a natural sex toy: it combines heat, pressure, moisture, and friction all in one device. According to *The Hite Report*, water massage using the shower is some women's favorite way of reaching orgasm.

GAMES
• Cover each other in liquid soap and give each other an erotic massage in the shower.
• Use the shower on an alternate pleasure/punishment basis. Pleasure means warm water directed at the genitals. Punishment is

a blast of cold water on the back.

• Have a combined bath and shower. Lie back in a hot, steamy, bath and use the flow of water from the shower hose to massage different parts of the body, such as the perineum, the genitals, the toes, the lips, the soles of the feet, and the backs of the knees.

• See if you can masturbate each other to orgasm using only the jets of water from the showerhead.

• Surprise your partner with some impromptu oral sex in the shower.

Shower sex positions

The best position for shower sex is one in which the woman bends over and the man penetrates her from behind. This is because, while you are standing on a slippery surface, each partner has the least likelihood of skidding halfway across the shower tray!

BUBBLES AND
Cuddles

Baths are the perfect place for sensual indulgence. Unplug the phone, light some candles, and turn the hot tap on. Now add bubbles and essential oils and slip into the warm and welcoming water with your partner.

THE JUG GAME

Sit facing each other. Now fill a jug with bath water and tell your partner to close his eyes. Pour the water onto him from a height. Start by pouring it around his shoulders and belly and then lift the jug higher and direct the stream onto his penis. Now give him the jug – it's his turn!

SEX IN THE BATH

It may be hard to manage intercourse in the average-sized bath, but that doesn't mean you can't both have an orgasm. Pour plenty of liquid soap, bath oil, or shower gel onto his penis and massage him to orgasm. Stimulate her clitoris with bath oil, your toes, and then your fingers, until you bring her to a nice slippery climax.

AFTERPLAY IN THE BATH

Lying back in a steaming bubble bath is an intimate way to relax after sex. If you have room, lie back in each other's arms.

FINISHING TOUCH

Add fizz to your bathwater with an effervescent bath bomb. These are fragrant balls of sodium bicarbonate and essential oils that literally explode in the water.

EROTIC
Foam Bath

The combination of sparkling foam with the slightly scratchy rasp of a soap applicator bombards the skin with an unusual, sensual experience. Lay your hands on a beach chaise longue and position it in a sheltered part of your yard on a very hot day. You will also need a large bowl of hot water, some fragrant shower gel and one of the newer nylon, multi-layered, liquid-soap applicators. Begin by blindfolding your partner to make the sensations more acute.

WASH HER FEET

Kneel on the chaise longue and rest her feet on your thighs. Squeeze water onto her feet and drizzle shower gel between her toes. Now start to wash and massage her feet and ankles with

the applicator. Start with the
tops of the feet, then the toes,
and then the soles. Use a firm
touch if she is ticklish (if she is extremely
ticklish, use your hands and start by enfolding
her foot firmly between your palms).

DRIP WATER ALONG HER BODY

Now immerse the applicator in hot water and make a trail of
droplets along the length of her body: up her calves and thighs
and over her belly and chest. Ask her for feedback.

Next, drizzle a line of shower gel along her body and start to
softly massage her with the applicator. Create as much foam as
you can so that her body is covered in soft meringue-like peaks.
While the foam prickles and pops, pour a tiny stream of massage
oil over and down the genitals. Then massage the genitals with
your hands using some of the strokes described on pages 188–9.

The overall sensation is of every individual pore of the body
prickling as if it is being tweaked and stroked. And hey, we
possess an awful lot of pores!

LOVE ON THE
Beach

This erotic fantasy takes place on a deserted beach in an exotic country such as India, Jamaica, or Thailand. Many people fantasize about sex on a far-off shore: the combination of a beautiful location, a hot climate, the relaxing nature of a holiday, and being seminaked can bring about intense sexual desire. This is one to read out loud to each other, preferably when you are lying side by side on recliners on white sands beside the blue sea with nothing and no one but a couple of palm trees nearby!

ON THE BEACH

The woman is a voyeur. She admires the man from a distance as he spreads his beach towel on the sand, walks down to the water, wades in, and starts to swim powerfully toward the waves. She is still watching him as he returns to his towel, rubs himself with oil and lies down on his back in the hot sun.

She decides to go to the water's edge, where she knows that the man can see her. Provocatively, she takes off her top and her skirt, drops them on the sand, and, wearing only a bikini bottom, wades out. Now she drifts luxuriously on her back, feeling the ripples lap over every tissue and every pore. She wants to be noticed but the man is feigning sleep, watching her secretly from behind his half-closed eye lids.

As she emerges from the water, she sees that his eyes are closed. As if by accident, she walks close enough to splash him with droplets of water. When this fails, she touches him gently and sees the flicker of a smile on his face. But he still says nothing. Taking the smile for a cue, she kneels astride him and caresses his burning hot body with her long damp hair. Lightly she touches his lips, earlobes, neck, and nipples, with her fingertips. He lies still and silent but is quietly becoming aroused.

The woman (who is still wet) lies on top of the man, stomach to stomach with her feet resting on his. The moisture from her skin combines with the suntan lotion on his to provide an oily slick between their two bodies. While he lies still, she

begins to move on top of him. She slides backward and forward across his frame, making the minute space between them poker-hot with her ceaseless action. The slippery friction rolls and slides, sucking and pressing every dip and swell of the sultry skin. Soon one skin merges with the other, so that it becomes impossible to define where one gliding, rolling, body ends and the other begins. The movement feels out of control, yet, as she slides over his body, she makes sure to slide down across his genitals as well as up across his abdomen and chest. The friction becomes unbearable, and the water and the oil and the heat fuse to create a sexual explosion.

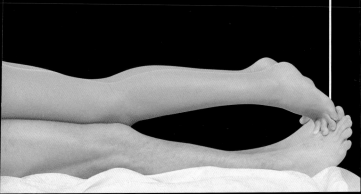

THE SHAMPOOING
Game

Prepare the bathroom in advance with candles, a bath full of fragrant hot water, and some big fluffy towels. Now lead your partner into the steamy bathroom and take off his clothes.

SENSUAL SHAMPOO

Ask him to step into the bath, lie back, and relax. Explain that you are going to start by washing his hair. Make every action as relaxing and sensual as possible. Ask him to tip his head back as you pour water and shampoo onto it and then give him a luxurious head massage, applying deep circular pressure with your fingertips, first at his temples, then along his hair-line and all over his scalp.

154

Next, take a comb and sensually comb his hair, running the teeth over his scalp, arousing the millions of tiny nerve-endings which lie beneath the skin. When he steps out of the bath, wrap him in warm fluffy towels, and seat him in front of a large mirror. Standing behind him, take out a pair of scissors.

If he has a beard or a moustache, now is the time for trimming. The act of clipping and cutting sends sensual tickles up to the scalp and down the rest of the torso. If he doesn't possess facial hair, make it appear as if you are going to cut the hair on his head. There's something about a woman wielding cold steel next to the skin that turns men on.

THE PELVIC SHAMPOO

Wash his genital area, including his scrotum and perineum. Swirl your finger tips lightly in and out of his most intimate crevices, explaining all the time that he is a very dirty boy down there and must submit to being properly cleaned.

155

STEAM ROOMS AND
Saunas

Steam rooms and saunas have long enjoyed a sexy reputation and are often the scene of great sexual arousal. The steamy tropical temperatures and low lighting give them a moody atmosphere that's always been conducive to sexy thoughts and fantasies.

ENJOY A TROPICAL TREAT

Treat yourself and your partner to a day out at a health club or sports center, drifting between the sauna, steam room and jacuzzi. This is an excellent mood-lifter that helps you to unwind, have fun, and spend intimate time with your partner. It's especially luxurious during the cold winter months, and a good way to get in the mood for sex.

Jacuzzi therapy

Jacuzzis are specially designed tubs with massaging jets of water that pummel your body. Being immersed in warm bubbling water has a sensual and therapeutic effect on the body. Water increases your circulation, relaxes tight muscles, lowers blood pressure, and makes your skin feel alive and glowing. If you position your partner so that the genitals are in line with the bubbles, you can bring him or her to climax this way.

SAUNA AND STEAM ROOM TIPS

Try these ideas for a sensual time in the sauna, but don't be tempted to risk actual sex unless you are *very* discreet:

• suck on a mint. It won't cool you down, but you may feel as though you can breathe more easily

• massage coconut oil into each other's hair

• inhale cool and fresh smelling essential oils such as eucalyptus, grapefruit, or peppermint

• rub natural products into your partner's skin. Try papaya flesh on the face and honey on the body.

157

SEX IN THE
Sea

Sea water offers amazing buoyancy and supports body weight easily. This means that you can lift each other up and wind yourself into fantastic contortions with the greatest of ease. Some of the most impossible sex positions from the *Kama Sutra* are easily achieved out there in the ocean. The only problem that you may encounter is shifting sand. If sex in the

sea is simply too public, just wait a while until everyone has gone home, then make love on the sand dunes. Sand not only preserves heat; it molds itself to the exact shape of your body.

SAND GAMES

Instead of building sandcastles, do the adult equivalent:

- play hide and seek – find a secluded venue for sex and wait to be found
- draw sexy pictures in the sand
- mold her breasts or his penis in the sand
- play kiss tag.

SWIMMING POOL SEX

Most public pools frown on any type of horseplay, so synchronous sex games must be confined to your own private pool. If you have one, you might enjoy acting out the Frog. In the Frog, your lover stands with his back against the pool wall while you wrap your legs around his waist, feet against the wall, pushing off, and floating back. The flotation that you achieve means that your lover can support your weight while you perform pliés against him. The Chinese liken this movement to the mating of two frogs.

DINING WITH A
Difference

Our lips are a primary source of erotic
pleasure and since the beginning of time,
humans have found food sexy. Food can
be a sexual hors d'oeuvre, a sex aid, an
aphrodisiac, or an erotic feast for the
eyes. You may revel in whipped cream
spread out over your lover's body, or
enjoy sampling your favorite morsels
against their skin.

GAMES FOR
Gourmets

Sex and eating seem to have always gone hand in hand. Offering your partner food is an act of caring, and it plays a big part in courtship. Buying or cooking a meal for a partner remains a traditional offering of love, intimacy, and romance, and one that often precedes sexual intimacy. Playing with food, finding little games for lovers, fuels erotic feelings. In this little manual we take food and sex those few steps further, showing you unforgettably sexy gourmet experiences and giving you ideas of things to do with food that will blow your mind!

FOOD AND SEX

Did you ever think of combining sex and eating? Both are sensual activities that gratify some of our most compelling desires. Feeding each other with your fingers can turn into part of foreplay. You might cover your lover with food as part of a unique sexual banquet, or miraculously transform certain food items into innovative sex toys. Although giving and sharing

food is essentially a nurturing activity, food-sex games in adult-hood can take on any tone you want: childish, silly, intimate, outrageous, provocative, romantic, lustful, or sexy. Be inventive and imaginative – start looking at food in terms of its erotic potential. Go to the supermarket and buy exotic foreign foods that will give you fresh ideas for erotic eating.

Did you know?

According to folklore, women in Turkish harems were forbidden cucumbers unless they were fully sliced first.

163

FEEDING EACH
Other

Feeding is a nurturing activity that can awaken memories of being looked after as a child. Cook a delicious meal for your partner and actually put the titbits into each other's mouth. Feeding someone with your fingers is sexier than with a fork, so only use cutlery if you have to. Let the juices of the food run over your hands and mouth and indulge yourself in the sensuality of eating. You can clean up later. Take time to really savor what you are eating and describe the flavors and textures to each other.

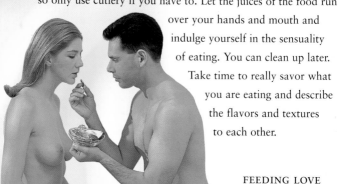

FEEDING LOVE
Feeding each other is a good way of showing that you really care.

THE STARTER

Choose foods that you can pick up in your fingers, such as baby mushrooms, asparagus, or artichoke prepared in butter; anything that tastes good and leaves a sensual gloss on your lips.

THE MAIN COURSE

Again, dispense with cutlery and use foods that are you can pick up, such as chicken legs, sausages, little potatoes, and long green beans. Alternatively, noodles and chopsticks are great fun.

THE DESSERT

Sensual fruits – particularly small, red, juicy berries, are the ideal dessert foods to feed to your partner. Try strawberries, raspberries, and red grapes. Fruits with fragrant and sticky juices such as plums, nectarines, ripe pears, and peaches are perfect pre-kissing fruits that will make you taste delicious.

The spaghetti game

Spaghetti is fun food to feed with. Use really long spaghetti, put one end in your mouth and one end in your partner's mouth – now suck.

EXPERIMENTING WITH
Aphrodisiacs

An aphrodisiac is any substance that increases sexual desire, arousal or performance. A vast range of substances have earned a reputation for being aphrodisiacs. Some, such as Spanish fly and yohimbine, cause dangerous side effects. Others, such as rhino horn, are simply ineffective. But the majority of food aphrodisiacs are harmless and, according to experts, they often work because we believe in their sensual powers.

OYSTERS AND CHAMPAGNE

Treat yourself and your lover to a midnight feast of oysters and champagne. Oysters are reminiscent of the female genitals. They are also rich in zinc, which may contribute to the health of the reproductive organs. Champagne, with its bubbles and heady perfume, is the drink of celebration. Caviar or mussels are just as good as oysters, or try asparagus tips dipped in butter.

Inflame Your Lover's Senses

Cook a spicy meal and share it with your lover. However, be careful with chillies – if you touch skin after handling them it will sting, and they can even cause blindness if you rub your eyes with your fingers after cutting them. The good news is that hot spices have long had a reputation as aphrodisiacs, probably because they raise body temperature, increase heartbeat, and flush the skin.

GINSENG

Share a cup of tea using fresh ginseng root. Some people believe it boosts your libido. The word "ginseng" means "man root," and it is traditionally used as an energizing tonic in Eastern cultures. Don't take ginseng if you have high blood pressure.

CHOCOLATE AND TURKISH DELIGHT

Give your lover a gift of chocolate and Turkish delight. Both of these products contain a substance called phenyethylamine (PEA), which people produce naturally when they are infatuated with another person.

HANKY PANKY
Picnic

Make sure that the setting for your picnic is secluded. The last thing you want is a group of hikers stumbling across you as you serve an intimate dessert to your partner!

THE HANKY PANKY PICNIC BASKET

Pack a picnic basket full of picnic foods – the more luxurious the better. The aim is to be as adventurous as possible. Start

The shopping list:
- French bread
- cold meats or a selection of dips
- a cucumber
- some carrots
- caviar and crackers
- a watermelon
- some frozen grapes in a thermos
- figs
- oranges
- papaya
- champagne
- lollipops
- condoms.

your picnic by spreading out a huge sheet. Then unpack the food. Ideally, it should contain some of the items listed in the ideal shopping list on the opposite page.

BE PROVOCATIVE

Eat the food as provocatively as you can. Don't worry about choosing sweet foods before savory – just eat whatever you like. Make bite-sized sandwiches and feed them to each other. Put a frozen grape between your teeth and offer it to your partner (or drop it down her top "by accident"). Share the same piece of watermelon, and then kiss the juice off each other.

SEXUAL
Banquet

The sexual banquet is unique in that there are no tables, chairs, knives, or forks. Your partner's naked body is the plate upon which the food is served, and you are the sole diner. Other essential ingredients are a can of whipped cream, a pot of honey or syrup, and a selection of soft, juicy fruits.

Sex banquet tips

• Ask your partner to "hide" a dab of honey on his body. Your job is to find it with your tongue.

• Use a new paintbrush to paint the body with runny foods such as cream, ice cream, syrup, yogurt, or custard.

• Let your sexual banquet degenerate into mayhem and have a food fight. Smother each other in whipped cream, crush fruit into his hair, and pour custard all over her.

• Eat a whole meal from your partner's body. Arrange the starter on the chest, the main course on the belly, and the dessert on the abdomen and genitals.

STIMULATE THE BODY WITH FOOD

Use food to stimulate your partner's body. Aim for subtle
stimulation at first – slowly drip honey from a spoon into the
navel, squeeze fresh orange juice onto the skin, run an ice cube
over the nipples, lick chocolate sauce from the neck or, using
whipped cream, make a pattern on the body and then lick it off.

As your partner begins to get aroused, start to stimulate the
genitals in an indirect way. For example, dribble champagne
between her legs or place a bagel around his penis and nibble it,
being sure to brush his penis "accidentally" with your tongue.

FANTASY
Picnic

In this fantasy role play, the woman is completely vulnerable and the man takes charge of the whole sexual encounter. How you enact this fantasy is up to you. You can either pick and choose the elements that you want to recreate at home or, if you can be sure of privacy, you can go on a real picnic in the forest.

THE FANTASY SETTING

Imagine that you are alone at a picnic in a clearing in a forest. You have eaten some of the food from your picnic basket and you decide to lie back and savor the sounds and smells of the forest. It is a hot day, and you take your clothes off so that you can feel the sensation of the sun on your skin. Thoughts of sex drift into your mind, but just as you are starting to caress yourself, you hear the sound of a twig snapping. You sit up, afraid that you are not

alone. You listen hard,
and you can make out
rustling sounds that
seem to be getting closer
and coming toward you.

Before you have a chance to act, a
man appears in the clearing. He is
someone you vaguely recognize but do not
know well. In stark contrast to your nakedness,
the man is dressed formally in a three-piece suit.
The man has an air of respectability that seems
out of place with the scene and your nudity.
You are embarrassed and try to cover
your breasts with your hands.

But the man shows no hint of disapproval or even
surprise. He opens his case and pulls out an
immaculate white tablecloth that he spreads out on
the forest floor. He tells you to lie down on the
tablecloth while he pulls the picnic basket over
toward you. Slowly and meticulously, the stranger

arranges all the food from the basket on your naked body. Then, he casually sits back to admire his work.

THE FEAST

Your mood is slowly turning from nervousness to interest. You want to know what is going to happen next, and you are starting to feel aroused. Slowly the man stands up, takes his jacket off, folds it neatly, and places it on the ground. Then he tucks a white napkin into his shirt. All of his movements are mannered and precise.

He tells you to stay absolutely still so that none of the food falls off and then he kneels beside you and begins to eat from your body. He licks cream cheese and raspberries from your chest and, by the time he gets to your genitals, the chocolate that he has placed there is beginning to melt. As a result he starts to lick your clitoris. You realize that, despite his composure, he has an erection. Yet he has made no attempt to move inside you. This is curiously sexy. You find you begin to respond and very quickly the pressure from his tongue becomes so amazing that you start to writhe and moan until, eventually, even though you try, you cannot prevent your orgasm.

GAME ANALYSIS

The man is the dominant partner but he dominates by looks, actions, and gestures, rather than actual commands. Toward the climax of the scenario, the man is obviously very aroused, but he never loses control. The woman, meanwhile, starts by playing innocent – she tries to hide her growing arousal – but in the end she gives in.

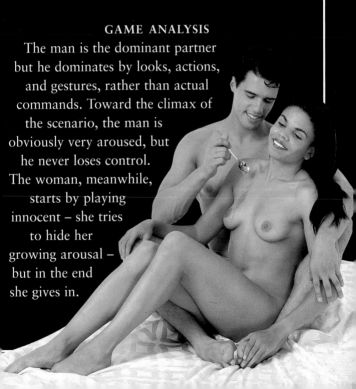

X-RATED
Games

This part of the book is cautiously rated
for the supermature only. It is a kind
of masterclass in the art of giving oral
pleasure which extends to teaching
superlative genital massage. Such hand
and mouth masterstrokes might be used
during spontaneous sex, or you may
consider them prizes to be awarded for
good behavior during any sex game.

EXTREME GAMES FOR
Sexperts

Rewards, in the form of the x-rated strokes demonstrated throughout this chapter, can be prizes for good behavior. But they can also be used as an instrument of torture. For example, just when your man is groaning with delight as you offer him oral sex, you might slowly withdraw.

Perhaps in some sympathy, you return to your pleasure-giving task. But then he will twitch a hand or attempt to stroke your hair. You halt the proceedings immediately. He will be enraged and half-afraid. He doesn't know now if you intend to finish what you've started. This version of Punishment and Reward can run on and on.

Alternatively, you might apply your most cunning manual arts to his straining body. Only now the game orders him to resist climax at all costs, otherwise he pays a massive forfeit. Usually, the end result is a great orgasm.

ORAL SEX
For Him

A woman's mouth is small and her man's penis is usually rather larger. The secret to good oral sex is discovering how to make each complement the other so that he feels truly engulfed and she resists feeling suffocated.

THE STARTING POINT

Don't wait until your man has an erection before applying your mouth to him. Take him into your mouth while he's still soft and partially suck on him and partially swallow. The swallowing movement makes a distinct pull on his penis and creates a pressure. If you do it rhythmically, his erection will take shape.

TONGUE SHAPING

Holding his penis at the base with one hand, run your pointed tongue up one side of his penis, across the top and, when you go down the far side let the underneath of your tongue take the strain. Do this two or three times before going on to use your tongue like a sculpting tool, literally licking his penis into shape.

RUNNING AROUND IN CIRCLES

Now push your mouth down on his penis so that it begins to penetrate further into your mouth and then retreat again. As you do this, setting up a rhythm, circle your tongue around and around the head of his penis, so that his manly member is being subjected to two separate strokes and counter-rhythms at the same time. This is tremendously stimulating for him.

TWANGING THE GUITAR

As you hold his penis in your mouth, flick your pointed tongue backward and forward across the top of his penis where the frenulum (the long ridge that runs the length of his penis) is situated. It's a bit like twanging a guitar string. And when you feel he's enjoyed enough flicking, try humming. The humming vibrates his entire penis, and every time you change the tone or the pitch of the hum he experiences it differently.

THE EXTENDED MOUTH

Now comes the secret maneuver for women with small mouths. Once the head of his penis is in your mouth,

place your wet hand around his penis but up against your lips so that it feels to him as if your lips have extended and completely enclosed his penis. Now, as your mouth goes up and down on his penis, make sure that your hand accompanies the movement.

VARYING THE PRESSURE

Your finger and thumb will naturally meet around his penis and you might try varying their pressure. Older men often need a much greater pressure to get any distinct sensation, while younger men simply enjoy the contrast. Don't be afraid to squeeze quite hard.

ORAL SEX
For Her

The tongue is probably the world's greatest sex aid, since it gives gorgeous variation of sensation directly onto the clitoris while simultaneously making it so wet that it feels as if you can just slide straight inside.

SWORD PLAY

For really sensational cunnilingus, your head needs to be right between her thighs and preferably slightly below them, so that you can stroke your tongue upward against the shaft of her clitoris. From here you can also occasionally insert your tongue into her vagina.

Tactile tips

Never bite the clitoris, although a few gentle nibbles on the labia can be sensational. If you get a cramp in your jaw, don't give up on the cunnilingus. Try keeping your tongue still, but move your head up and down instead.

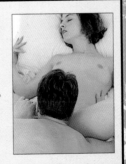

TONGUE STROKES

• With a featherlight pressure, twirl your tongue around the very top of the clitoris.

• Flick the tip of your tongue from side to side underneath the clitoris.

• Cover the clitoris with your mouth, sucking gently (not hard, otherwise you will bruise her), and flick your tongue across it at the same time.

• While continuing to twirl or flick, put a finger into her vagina and pull gently downward.

X-RATED MASSAGE
For Him

There are some amazing genital massages for men that offer such explosive variation of sensation that you begin to wonder why anyone bothers with straightforward intercourse.

THE METRONOME

This can be done with a partially soft penis. In it, you prop the penis up with one hand and give it a little push toward the other, which catches it after it has moved only a couple of inches. This other hand then pushes it back to the first one again. Keep this up, and the penis is eventually clocking backward and forward like the pointer on a metronome. It's an excellent method for turning your guy on.

HAND OVER HAND

Using your hands as rings, slide one ring down your man's shaft, rapidly followed by the other. As one hand reaches the base of the penis, bring it up and start at the top again.

THE LEMON SQUEEZER

Holding the penis upright with one hand, gently rub the palm of the other hand across the top of the head.

THE JUICER

Hold the penis upright with one hand and, shaping the fingers of your other hand so that they point downward in a kind of spider shape, lightly grasp the head of the penis with this "spider" and twist your fingers backward and forward around the head as if you were juicing a lemon.

Action tip

Never do any genital massage without using tons of scented lubrication. The easier you let your hands wander across your partner's genitals, the greater the sensation and general comfort he will enjoy.

X-RATED MASSAGE
For Her

The skin is the body's biggest organ, and just beneath its surface lie millions of tiny nerve endings all sensitive to touch. Few parts of the human body are more sensitive than the female genitals, so here now are some powerful rewards in the shape of wonderful touch strokes for them.

DUCK'S BILL

Shape the fingers of one hand into a "duck's bill," hold them above her clitoris, and pour warmed massage oil over them so that it slowly seeps through and runs onto her genitals, but not into her vagina. This is experienced as a flooding sensation, full of warmth but slightly disturbing – which is as it should be.

"WIBBLING"

Start with the outer labia. Use both of your hands at the same time, gently pull on it, then let go, just as you might do if this were one of the lips of your

Safety tips

Oil stains, so make quite sure your partner is lying on a bed of towels. Please ensure that the oil is warm and that it doesn't flow inside her vagina.

mouth. When you've "wibbled" one outer lip, repeat the process on the other, and then move on to the inner lips.

CLITORAL MANEUVERS

Extremely delicately, with an almost featherlight touch and using plenty of lubrication, run your finger first around the head and then up and down the shaft of her clitoris.

HAPPY
Anniversaries

Those of us who live in cities tend to lose sight of the natural progression of the seasons. We don't notice that there is variety out there in the natural world. But one way of paying attention to some of life's natural variations is by consciously deciding to celebrate some of life's high points. This is where anniversaries come in.

GAMES FOR SPECIAL
Times

The 21st-century method of offering variation
to our lives is to focus on celebrating
anniversaries, be they personal or cultural.
We make a big deal out of giving presents,
throwing dinner parties, going out for drinks,
or spending celebratory time with friends and
family. We tend not to use sex for these events,
because most of us feel that sex, to be good
and to feel "real," ought to be spontaneous.

What we sometimes lose sight of is that we
often spend hours thinking about sex, running
it through our heads in fantasy. What happens
at the end of this process still falls under the
title of "spontaneous," because in spite of this
unconscious brainstorming we still don't
actually know what will happen. How can

we? What eventually takes place depends on another person. And other people are unpredictable. Aren't they?

OFF TO THE NIGHTCLUB

Of course, other people are unpredictable. But even then there are a few things that you can foresee. If you delight your woman with a romantic Valentine's supper for two, the odds are she'll adore you for it. If you celebrate your manfriend's birthday by sweeping him off to a transsexual nightclub, he will most likely be thrilled. On the next few pages I discuss some of the more significant anniversaries, the ones that we celebrate "en masse" and some that are more personal.

> *Action tip*
> Be sensitive to your partner's preferences, but don't be afraid of having some special celebrations on High Days and Holidays.

YOUR *Birthday*

The sex game picked for a birthday celebration ought to be something particularly personal to your partner. For example, one man knew his woman was fascinated by androgynous individuals. So he invited her to a cross-dressing party – for two. He took great pains with his appearance, shaved his legs, arranged his hair (which was conveniently long), put on a dress and carefully applied makeup. She, fascinated, fell in with the theme with enthusiasm and arrived wearing a tailored pinstriped pantsuit, hair slicked back, her face minus makeup.

The meeting was momentous. She took one look at him, slammed the front door shut, didn't stop to think about the supper carefully laid out, but just grabbed her man and carted

194

him off to the bedroom. He only had time to hiss "keep it in character" before she fell on him in a frenzy.

HINTS FOR HER

Get into the idea that it is up to you to make the moves. If he likes the idea, you can penetrate him with a finger or with a small vibrator. Or if you consider yourself to be a real boundary-breaker, you might invest in a strap-on dildo and truly get into character.

HINTS FOR HIM

Pamper your woman until she is out of her mind with sensual pleasure. Prepare a sweet-smelling bath for her, slowly and luxuriously soak her, feed her luscious fruit, and give her champagne from a tall, ice-cold, fluted glass. Then wrap her in hot, fluffy towels and carry her to bed.

And when it's all over? Well naturally you cut the birthday cake.

RELATIONSHIP
Anniversary

By definition, an anniversary is the celebration of a long time spent together. A very special method of spicing up your long-term relationship therefore is to play at the game of First Meeting.

THE GAME

In First Meeting you pretend that you are making each other's acquaintance for the first time. Arrive separately at a restaurant for dinner and sit at separate tables. As you order your meal, "notice" the other person at a nearby table. Keep on noticing. Eventually one of you might walk over to the other and introduce yourself or you might send a note over via the waiter, saying how you have been unable to tear your eyes away. The other might choose this moment to look coy.

196

Thank you very much, they might indicate, directly or through the waiter, but I don't normally do this kind of thing.

But you still can't seem to stop your eyes from swiveling in this person's direction. Eventually, you ask the waiter to take a drink over to the other's table. Now it is up to the other whether or not to say, "Thank you very much, come on over and talk."

GAME ANALYSIS

Perhaps this doesn't sound like much of a game when you read the idea in black and white, but the experience of acting it out under the eyes of other people – knowing that the waiter, for example, truly thinks you are picking each other up – can be curious. It is as if it is really happening. You wonder what the waiter thinks about you. Or if anyone else in the room has even noticed and perhaps disapproves. Try it and see.

VALENTINE'S *Day*

Plan on a private celebration. Invite your partner over to your place for the evening and meet him at the door with a bottle of champagne. While you are loosening up to the accompaniment of champagne bubbles and some prime sound, feed your lover a light Valentine's supper. Wait on him and agree to every request he makes. When he is finished, tell him that you will treat him to the best thing on earth to help digest his meal. Take him over to an armchair, take his shoes off, and give him a soothing foot massage as he relaxes.

THE PAMPERED FOOT

Using liquid soap (peppermint for added zest) kneel in front of him and, cradling his feet in warm towels, massage first one, then the other foot. Tell your partner to close his eyes

throughout and on no account help in any way by moving his limbs. All such movement is your responsibility. The experience for the person being pampered is of helplessness, luxury, and trust.

When he is so relaxed that he is a complete pussycat, end your massaging and walk him through to the bedroom. Now try out some of the grown-up stuff on him. See pages 186–7 for our X-rated strokes. The idea is that this is his special Valentine treat. This is a time devoted entirely to him. Your needs can be looked after at another time.

FANTASTIC FOOT STROKES

With both hands holding one foot, press your thumbs firmly into the sole of the foot and rotate firmly on the surface. Repeat all over the bottom of the foot. Slip a well lubricated finger between two toes and slowly pull it backward and forward. Repeat between the other toes.

MAY
Day

May Day is an original Bacchanalian, priapic festival celebrating wine and sex. In ancient days a giant phallus was paraded down the streets followed by laughing, drinking men and women. After the parade, many of the revelers would retreat into the bushes for their own form of celebration. So extreme were some people's antics that one Roman emperor actually banned the celebrations in order to preserve the public peace. Remember all that medieval maypole dancing? Did you know that it is a leftover of the earlier, wilder festival? Here's what you can do to bring this phallic anniversary up to date.

THE GAME

Tell your partner that you have been asked by a sex toys' manufacturer to test market some of their apparates. Handle the game clinically. Ask your partner to lie back on the bed, having removed their panties/boxer shorts, and ask your partner to rate each piece of equipment as either a) satisfactory, b) highly satisfactory, or c) not satisfactory at all. Then systematically test out the largest range of vibrators you can lay your hands on. You might experiment with a ring-shaped vibrator that fits around the base of the penis, an electric powered giant that shakes the whole body, let alone the penis, or the special anal model that is curved slightly in order to reach the super-sensitive prostate area. Make sure you keep to the role to ensure that the experience is more provocative.

DISCRETION ASSURED

If you hate the idea of visiting a sex shop in person for your vibrators, try virtual shopping on the internet. See the Appendix for our useful websites.

THANKSGIVING
Sex Games

The Thanksgiving meal commemorates the feast given in thanks for a safe harvest by the Pilgrim colonists in 1621, and has become an important part of American life. Each year, families all over America sit down together to a huge meal of roast turkey and other anniversary fare to give thanks. There are many other reasons, however, to give thanks. Perhaps you have a special event to celebrate. You have passed an important exam. Or maybe landed a new job. There are many exciting life occasions when we want to do something special.

One couple decided to serve each other up as the Thanksgiving feast! Mara trussed George up like a turkey, tying his arms and legs loosely together. Once he was lying on his back with his limbs strapped across him, Mara rubbed George down with oil, actually basting him with teaspoonfuls of the stuff. She decided against putting him in the oven, but substituted a powerful hair dryer so that she might heat certain meaty portions. This all felt so silly that George spent much of the time convulsed with laughter. The denouement came when the "bird" was considered ready for eating. Mara fell on him and pretended to chomp all over. The couple laughed so much that when Mara finally unstrapped him, they laughed all the way to climax. Laughter raises adrenaline levels, as do other forceful emotions. Raised adrenaline levels mean the sexual response cycle has already begun! It makes a nice change to turn on to humor.

TACTFUL TIP
Only play this game with someone whom you know possesses exactly the same sense of humor as yourself!

CHRISTMAS/CHANUKAH
Sex Fun

Ho, ho, ho! What is it that comes to mind as we think about Christmas? Santas, holly, brightly wrapped gifts, roaring fires, the Yule log? And although Chanukah does not have the same connotations, some of the Christmas razzmatazz has gotten mixed up with the Jewish festival because they are situated so close together. Bright lights, the cold, and roaring fires are certainly common to both festivals. In order to get fully into the spirit of yule, I suggest a hands-on present in the shape of a "hot" massage.

You might prepare your lover for their present by giving them an envelope. Inside is a beautifully penned certificate saying "This certificate entitles you to one 'hot' massage." The hotter the better you might think, as you struggle against the icy seasonal weather.

HOT MASSAGE

Hot massage consists of ordinary body massage, but done with a special massage cream. The best sort to use is a muscle rub cream, some of which can be bought through mail order or the internet (see Appendix). If you are into seriously intense sensation, you might think about a strong muscle rub, but be aware, if you apply too much of this it can actually burn. Give your partner the hottest massage of their life, barring the genitals. When it comes to paying attention to those organs, wash your hands and switch to X-rated strokes.

For her, you might try lightly circling on her clitoris, or gently tugging tiny clumps of her pubic hair. For him, you might try the "countdown" massage on his penis – massaging *down* the shaft of the penis ten times, then *up* the shaft ten times. Repeat nine times, then eight, seven, and six times through to once – if he can hold out for that long!

LUCKY
Dip

Perhaps it's one of those dull gray days when you can't believe anything nice is ever going to happen again and summer feels a long way off. Nor are there any pleasant anniversaries or treats to look forward to. It's a day, in fact, for the Lucky Dip. This is an invention designed to shake you and your partner out of your winter blues – look in the lucky dip bag and get into a more festive state of mind.

STAGE ONE

Get out the Dip Bag. This can be any kind of bag. In the bag are a number of sex commands written on separate pieces of paper. If you don't happen to have such a Dip Bag conveniently lying around your house, you might enjoy preparing one in advance, just in case of exactly this type of rainy day! What

206

sort of sex commands should you give? Here
are some suggestions:

• hot and cold oral sex, alternating your
mouth heated by hot tea with your mouth
cooled by ice cubes
• exchanging fantasies
• acting like a horny lesbian
• pretending you are a hooker
• vice cop
• applying for a job.

STAGE TWO
Obey the commands.

GAME ANALYSIS
Lucky Dip sounds horribly artificial and may
inspire you to run a mile. The interesting thing,
however, about doing sexual things because
you've been "told to," is that sometimes they
turn out to be very sexy indeed. This is
probably because the "telling" somehow gives
you permission to be a very different person.

THE
Passive Male

First, choose your man carefully before trying this scenario. Not every male is capable of being passive – even if only for half an hour. Build up your sex pattern slowly. Invite him over to your place after work for a drink. When he arrives, kiss him, keep on kissing him, and allow your bodies to settle on the couch, the floor, even the kitchen table – anywhere, as long as you can stretch out, preferably all over him.

If he struggles to reciprocate, soothe him by saying, "No, just lie back and enjoy. This is a present for you. It's all for you." When his melting body is showing signs of wanting to merge with yours, take his clothes off. Quickly, deftly, remove his shirt, unzip his pants, and strip them off, then take off your own clothes. This just leaves him in his briefs.

Kissing and biting down the length of his torso, let your hands work their way inside his briefs, then casually peel them off. Now, begin performing oral sex on him. With your lips covering your teeth, nibble at the sensitive ridge along the underside of his penis, flutter the tip of your tongue over the head of it, suck on it as though it were an ice cream cone, and swirl your fingers around the base. If he hasn't gotten an erection when you start these moves, he soon will.

Next, move up from his genitals and press kisses onto his cheeks, his temples and the sides of his mouth before allowing your lips to fasten onto his. Run your tongue around the inside of his mouth, and while he is flooded with pleasure and aching with desire, slide your vagina carefully onto his erection and enclose him tightly. Now drive him on to a dramatic climax. Pull up above him quite slowly, brushing his chest or even his face with your breasts, then thrust firmly down again. You are setting the pace, sending him out of his mind with pleasure, riding up and down the full length of his penis, and forcing him into a spectacular orgasm.

TAKING THINGS FURTHER
Making love to someone who is passive yet supremely responsive can be absolutely addictive. The trouble with this is that it drives you on to take risks. One friend told me that she used to drag her manfriend into dark doorways in remote parts of town and force him to have sex with her (not that he objected that much, of course!) But this kind of behavior is definitely not to be recommended. If you want to behave outrageously, just make sure you do it in private, away from anyone else.

BEDTIME
Stories

Reading your lover a story at bedtime is
an act of pure indulgence – it's a time-
honored method of offering a special treat.
Perhaps the stories are sexually arousing in
themselves. Or perhaps they just lay the
groundwork for relaxation and mutual
approval. Here are two stories that you
can recount to your partner just before
you lure them under the bedclothes.

THE UNSPUN VERSION
Cinderella

Ella, her stepmother Jane, and her two stepsisters, Candy and Lulu, were in a fluster. They had just received an invitation to the Royal Ball. The problem was that today was Friday, and the ball was on Saturday. "What on earth to wear!", was the first question that sprang to mind.

Since Jane's husband (and Cinderella's father) had died, money had been very tight. It's not easy for four women to survive on a small retirement income. However, some clever rustling around in their mutual wardrobes, plus a great deal of exchanging of garments, ended up with all four women meeting the challenge and managing to look stunning for the ball. The only items that they had to buy specially for the event were the masks that would disguise them.

On the night of the ball Jane persuaded Ella's godmother, Mary, to lend them her coach, and the all-female family arrived at the palace in style. Thanks to the overtight bodice style of the time, the women had no difficulty in securing dancing partners. Indeed, such was the whirl of the ballroom that Ella several times lost sight completely of her stepmother and two sisters.

Ella had of course met the prince before. His family and hers were old friends but she hadn't seen him for some years. During that time he had acquired a reputation as a bit of a playboy. "Not really my type," Ella had explained to Jane. "Anyway he feels like a brother."

Toward 11 o'clock Ella was approached by a tall, dark, and handsome man (also masked) whom she assumed to be one of the prince's college friends. This man was a different kettle of fish altogether.

There was something about him that set her pulse soaring and turned her knees to jelly. It took only one waltz for Ella to feel like urgently going somewhere a little quieter. Fortunately, the stranger appeared to feel the same.

Ella found herself leading the young man toward the royal summer house, which she remembered well from childhood. Once inside, he pushed her against the rustic wall and kissed her so passionately that she almost forgot to breathe. Within an embarrassingly short time she had sunk onto a conveniently placed old mattress on the floor with her bodice pushed down to her waist, her panties tossed on the bench at the back and the prince's friend thrusting into her as if all hell depended on his strokes.

He was graced with an exceptionally large penis, and Ella almost immediately felt sensual tension mounting. In fact, a kind of turmoil engulfed her as he appeared to stimulate her from four different directions at once. One hand went down her pubis to her labia, and rubbed lubriciously and sensationally across her clitoris, while the other hand somehow crept around the back and slid a large finger into her back passage. This finger puzzlingly seemed to enlarge as he continued to move it. What with the powerful thrusting at the front and the contra thrusting at the back, not to mention the incredible stroking, Ella was at the very point of screaming her head off when she suddenly heard a clamor of voices outside.

"Ella, where are you? We've got to go. The coach is about to leave. Ella you must come at once," shouted her sisters as they hurried up the gravel walk towards the summer house. As Ella heard their voices, she also took in the unmistakable sound of the palace clock chiming midnight. Damn! Her godmother had made it quite clear that the coachman, who was an independent spirit with a mind of his own, would not wait a minute after midnight before setting off for home.

Screaming out, "Oh, Lord," and "I'm *so* sorry," and fueled by her now massive sexual tension, Ella shot out of the young man's embrace, hiked her bodice up over her large breasts and rushed to unlock the door. Astoundingly enough her mask was still in place. Slamming the door closed behind her so that her sisters couldn't see her appalled lover, she joined them in racing to the entrance. They actually made it to the carriage by the last stroke of the clock.

"You look a bit flushed," said Jane accusingly to Ella. "I met this gorgeous young man," said Ella dreamily, "one of the prince's friends I think." "Ah," said her companions with understanding. Each fell to her own silent thoughts.

The next day in church, the four women were a little surprised to hear it announced that the prince had met a beautiful young woman the previous night at the ball, whom he had utterly fallen for and intended to marry. This paragon of beauty had left in a hurry, and it was unfortunately only by an item of clothing that the prince would be able to identify her. That afternoon, every unmarried woman in town might expect a visit from him.

It wasn't until Ella unsuspectingly opened the front door to the prince that she realized what she had done. Admittedly she hadn't seen the man for years, but oh, how he had changed. With no difficulty at all she recognized him as the ardent lover of the previous night. Suddenly she didn't feel so uninterested after all.

But it was with embarrassment that she identified the panties she had so carelessly tossed aside in the summer house. "Would any of you charming ladies lay claim to these?" asked the prince with a twinkle in his eyes. Ella was poised to say blushingly "Oh dear, they are mine," when she received a shock.

"They are mine," said her stepmother, who daringly pulled up her skirt at the side to reveal that she was indeed wearing their twin. And, of course, they did belong to Jane. They were one of the many garments that the four relatives had tossed around during their excited and extensive preparations for the ball.

After many cries of joy had been uttered and the prince had plighted his troth to Jane, and after the royal party had left, promising to return again very soon, Ella received another shock.

"What do you mean by this?" she screamed at her stepmother as soon as the front door was closed.

"You know I was wearing those panties. You know I was with him last night."

As her stepmother looked at her oddly, Candy and Lulu joined in the screaming too. "What do you mean Ella?" they shrieked simultaneously, "we were with that man last night, in the summer house. We all wore the same panties. How dare you lay claim to him?"

Jane looked at all three girls with a cold fury. "You can all stop shouting," she declared icily, "I was with the prince last night. Those are my panties and I have no intention of sharing anything with you children any more ever again, especially not my next husband."

Oh well, Ella thought to herself, as her shock subsided. "You win some, you lose some – I never did like the prince very much anyway!"

THE
Love Game

"It's no use Tom, I'm going to have to withdraw from the competition." Alison sounded fed up.

"But why?" Tom felt himself surprisingly stung by disappointment.

"Because it's not possible for either of us to win. I've thought about it from every which way and each time I come up with... the impossibility of the task. If both of us know that each is trying to make the other fall in love, the equation cancels out. I honestly don't believe it's possible."

"But what about the prize money? What about the web video coverage? If you withdraw we lose the lot. Can't you try a little harder?"

"No," Alison was final. "I'm going to tell the organizers we are dropping out."

"Um," Tom was thoughtful. "We could just not tell them until the final broadcast. At least that way we'd get coverage and an ongoing fee. I really need the money, Ali."

Alison reconsidered. "You mean we would have to pretend?"

"It wouldn't kill us," Tom pointed out. "And it would pay the bills for three more months."

And so a working agreement was forged. In return for Tom's agreement to withdraw, Alison would refrain from resigning their place. In return for Tom's promise to keep quiet about her withdrawal, the couple would at least benefit from a small income while fooling the judges.

The Love Game had been announced on WebVid three months ago and hundreds of couples had immediately signed up for the competition. The goal was to make each other fall in love within a timescale of six months. The first person to succeed (in getting the other to turn starry-eyed) would be the winner. The trick (behind the webcam company's risk of shelling out millions) was that the task contained a built-in paradox. If you are told to fall in love, it is virtually impossible. So far there had been no winners but a lot of funny and despairing web coverage.

Once Tom and Alison had come to their private deal, the atmosphere between the couple lightened. Knowing that they weren't going to win and that none of their moves mattered any longer meant they could relax. However, to keep up appearances they did all the things that lovers traditionally do. They strolled in the woods, lunched by the side of the lake, held hands everywhere but, unlike most great lovers, their courtship was accompanied at every stage by a webcam.

Of course, they were entitled to turn the camera off. Nobody expected them to go to the bathroom while viewed by millions. And the need for privacy intensified as the months went by. Increasingly, the camera got switched off. During these blind periods Tom and Alison would slump side by side relaxing. The situation (off-camera) even became funny – a type of running joke.

Until one day, in a blind period, when Tom was fooling around as usual and Alison was convulsed with laughter, an unexpected thing happened. She kissed him. And he, taken by surprised, paused a minute and then sweetly and slowly kissed her back. Then it was as if a searing fire had swept over them. One minute they were a couple of kids, the next they were locked in an embrace.

"We've got to stop this," gasped Alison, her mouth full with Tom's lips. "It's against the rules."
"I can't," gasped Tom in return. "I can't wait a minute longer."

"Neither can I," she choked, and sank into him as if he were the ocean. Every move they made felt like sea foam, floating like bubbles lightly stroked by wavelets. After five months of touch abstinence, every inch of their skin and all the deep pockets of sensual tissue filled and swelled and grew until each caress was tinged with a pleasure so intense it was sharp. The pain pierced them and stilled them. Soon, with no movement at all, their bodies were transfixed by this soaring, aching delight.

They took each other's clothes off as if in slow motion. They lay together savoring the perfect texture of each other's nudity, touching, gliding, smoothly rubbing flesh on flesh. As their bodies slid and stroked and their cries murmured and mingled, they drove the other into greater layers of sensation. The build-up of perfect sensuality was like the slow detonation of a nuclear bomb. Layer grew upon layer, reaching higher and higher into the sky. Words tumbled out of their mouths with no meaning. The wonderful, aching, extraordinary sex pierced them through until the pleasure was shot through with pain, the roof lifted off the living room, and the couple mushroomed out into space.

Afterward: "It was only sex, wasn't it?" Alison's voice sounded unsure.

"Well, yes. Of course."

A pause. "Sex is against the rules though, isn't it?"

"Well yes," another pause.

The couple kissed passionately.

Another pause.

"What are we going to do?"

"Better not tell anyone, I suppose."

"No."

Ten minutes later. "Time to switch the camera on again."

"Kiss me first."

"I'd love to."

On the day of the finals, Alison and Tom concealed their shameful episode.

"Tom, we've got to tell them this hasn't worked."
"Shush," said Tom. "We'll fail the Love Test anyway. It doesn't matter."

Each couple stood in front of the Loveometer. The Loveometer is a lie detector that measures the couples simultaneously. On this occasion, both Tom and Alison stated that they were not in love with each other. And as they spoke, the Loveometer sounded the siren. According to the polygraph, they were both lying.

"Ladies and gentlemen, the winners," announced the host. "This couple is in love – it's official."
As Tom and Alison were garlanded and handed enormous checks, their every smile was transmitted all over the world. Afterward, without a camera dogging

their footsteps for the first time in six months, Tom rounded on Alison. "You fooled me, didn't you?," he sounded savage. "You got me to fall in love with you by announcing that there was no contest?"

Alison looked scared. "It's not true, Tom. If it were, I would have been spotted by the Loveometer. It must have been the sex."

Tom calmed down a bit. "Possibly. Let's see." Reaching out he took Alison in his arms. And fused into her marvelous body. Some half an hour later, he sat up again. "Yes," he agreed, "it must have been the sex." An arm snaked up and pulled him back down again.

Up on the ceiling a hidden eye transmitted everything. The competition organizers were not to be underestimated... They had recognized good webcam potential from the start.

EARLY WARNING
Systems

There are certain rules that should be obeyed during any sex game. For example, never tie anyone up and leave them for extended periods, and do not bring in any third parties to your sex life unless you and your partner have specifically agreed that this is acceptable.

Additionally, do not do anything that might offend members of the public, or is actually illegal, such as having sex in a park in mid-afternoon next to a children's playground.

The golden rule is: never force anyone to do anything they do not want to do. If you play S & M games, always agree, in advance, on a safety word, so that if the action gets too much, it can be easily stopped. If you don't want to do something, then say so. Do not hesitate to say "NO," even if you fear you might offend your partner and never obstruct the mouth and nose under any circumstances.

LOOKING GOOD, SMELLING GOOD

Most of us bathe and shower regularly, but how many of us pay serious attention to odors from our mouth and genitals? As a valuable general rule, if your genitals start smelling at all unpleasant and washing does not improve things, take yourself to your doctor or the nearest hospital. Genital infections are usually easy to treat and easy to clear up. But they sure can make admirers run a mile...

Mouth odor may mean that your gums need attention. So a trip to the dentist and the dental hygienist should clear that problem up. And a sweet-smelling mouth is vital. The mouth is about the first piece of human anatomy any of us gets close to.

ENJOYING
Safer Sex

Practicing safer sex is one of the most important ways in which you can help to protect yourself against a range of sexually-transmitted diseases (STDs), including HIV (human immuno-deficiency virus) and AIDS (acquired immune deficiency syndrome).

WHAT IS SAFER SEX?

Safer sex is any kind of sexual activity that does not involve the exchange of bodily fluids. When the penis penetrates the vagina during unprotected intercourse, the woman is exposed to the man's semen and he is exposed to her vaginal fluids. Since viruses and other infections may be transmitted in these fluids, this is a potentially risky activity. However, if either the man or the woman wear a condom, then neither partner is exposed to the other's fluids and risk is significantly reduced. If you and your partner are, or ever have been, intravenous drug users and you shared needles with other users, you need to adopt safer sex methods to ensure continued good health.

WHO SHOULD PRACTICE SAFER SEX?

Anyone who has concerns or doubts about the sexual health or history of a sexual partner should practice safer sex. Only if you both have a clean bill of sexual health and you have sex only with each other is it safe to avoid practicing safer sex.

THE PRINCIPLES OF SAFER SEX

• Use a condom during any kind of penetrative sex.

• Have non-penetrative sex. Activities such as caressing and massage are all low risk. Try mutual masturbation or oral sex using a condom.

TAKE CARE
Be sure of your partner before making love.

USING
Condoms

When it comes to protection against HIV, condoms are the safest form of contraception. There are many different types available: colored, flavored, textured, and even some that have special attachments. As long as the condom packet bears a recognized standard mark and a use-by date, you can be free to be experimental. Buy a selection of unusual condoms and try them out, giving each condom a rating.

KEEP THEM HANDY

Keep a condom underneath your pillow and slip it out at the critical moment. Hide condoms in secret places all over your house so that you can enjoy impromptu sex wherever you are.

SMOOTH APPLICATION

Develop a range of condom skills. Teach yourself to put them on slowly and quickly, in the dark, using only one hand. Practice makes perfect, and if you want a dummy penis to

work on, try a cucumber. Put a condom on your partner as you stimulate his penis with your hands and tongue. Try the old Thai trick of slipping the condom into your mouth so that you clad him in it as you bear down during oral sex.

GAMES

• Try out different methods for putting on condoms, depending on their color or flavor.

• Time your partner's speed at putting the condom on your penis.

• Tell her that she has got to break the world record in slipping a condom on so unobtrusively that you do not notice it.

Index

Acknowledgments

Editorial assistance: Kesta Desmond
Photography: Mark Harwood, Ranald MacKechnie, Paul Robinson, Jules Selmes
Additional photography: Steve Gorton
Picture credits: The publisher wishes to thank the following for their kind permission to reproduce copyright photographs: Ace Photo Agency: Colin Thomas 72–3, 93; Robert Harding Picture Library: 114–15; Doralba Picerno: 1, 24, 31; Pictor International: 112, 118; Rex Features: 123; Alexander Caminada 116; Tony Stone Images: Donna Day 136; Ralf Schultheiss 158; Telegraph Colour Library: Bay Hippsley 48, 140-1
Picture research: Angela Anderson
Props: *Ann Summers* for the loan of lingerie and sex aids.
Skin Two for the loan of pvc outfits.

For good quality sex aids try:

UK
Passion8
NES.,
PO Box 88
Hull HU5 5FW
Tel: 01482 873377

Ann Summers
For your nearest shop, or to organize a party, 'phone 020 8645 8320 or visit the website: www.annsummers.com

Skin Two (for pvc and bondage equipment)
Tel: 020 7735 7195.

US
Good Vibrations
1210 Valencia Street
San Francisco
CA 94110
Tel: (415) 974 8980
www.goodvibes.com

AUSTRALIA
The Tool Shed
Call (02) 9360 1100 or Toll Free on 1800 181 069 (outside Sydney) for your nearest shop in Sydney, or visit the website to view their selection of toys, accessories and clothing:
www.thetoolshed.com.au